Theodore A. Felch

FROM

POOR-HOUSE

TO

OR,

THE TRIUMPHS OF THE LATE

DR. JOHN KITTO,

FROM BOYHOOD TO MANHOOD.

A BOOK FOR YOUTH.

BY

WILLIAM M. THAYER,

AUTHOR OF "THE POOR BOY AND MERCHANT PRINCE," "LIFE AT THE FIRE SIDE," MORNING STAR," "PASTOR'S WEDDING GIFT," ETC., ETC.

E. O. LIBBY AND COMPANY,
BOSTON.
NEW YORK: C. SCRIBNER.
1859.

PRINTED BY

GEORGE C. RAND & AVERY.

STEREOTYPED BY J. E. FARWELL & CO

PREFACE.

WHEN a poor, deaf pauper, like Kitto, comes forth from his obsure condition, and rises, by his own personal exertions, to distinction among Biblical and Theological scholars, it is worth while to inquire *how it is done.* The young will be benefitted by studying such an example of perseverance. New and noble resolutions may be awakened thereby in their hearts, the fulfilment of which, may lead them on to usefulness and renown.

The subject of this volume, at fifteen years of age, was a deaf boy in the Poor-house. We endeavor to show what were the elements of his success, that young readers may learn how to triumph over the obstacles in their pathway. In order to prove that certain elements of character are necesssary to success in every calling, as well as to make the book more attractive to the young, numerous anecdotes from the lives of other men, particularly those who were deprived of one or more of the five senses, are introduced. Here an ample field is open, relating to the severest trials and privations that ever darkened human experience. If youth thus afflicted have overcome all difficulties in their way, and won for themselves an honorable place among the worthies of the past and present, surely those who are subject only to the more common and lesser privations of life, may not be disheartened

The volume need not be limited to youthful readers. Young men, on the threshold of life's sterner duties, will find on these humble pages, some eminent examples of success, that may nerve them for manly effort in their chosen pursuits.

W. M. T.

CONTENTS.

CHAPTER I.

SUTTON-POOL.

CHAPTER II.

HIS GRANDMOTHER.

CHAPTER III.

A CHANGE.

CHAPTER IV.

FEARFUL CALAMITY.

CHAPTER V.

PAINS BRING GAINS.

CHAPTER VI.

A STEP HIGHER.

CHAPTER VII.

THE POOR-HOUSE.

CHAPTER XI.

A HARD MASTER.

CHAPTER XII.

HIS SECOND STUDY.

CHAPTER XIII.

A COMPARISON.

CHAPTER XIV.

INCIDENTS.

CHAPTER XV.

YOUNG MASSIEU.

CHAPTER XVI.

ONWARD AND UPWARD.

CHAPTER XVII.

TWO IMPORTANT IDEAS.

CHAPTER XVIII.

DENTIST AND PRINTER.

CHAPTER XIX.

BIRTHDAYS.

CHAPTER XX.

FOUR OTHER QUALITIES.

CHAPTER XXI.

A MISSIONARY.

CHAPTER XXII.

PUBLICATIONS.

CHAPTER XXIII.

IMPOSSIBILITIES.

CHAPTER XXIV.

THREE MORE EXAMPLES.

CHAPTER XXV.

MORAL AND RELIGIOUS CHARACTER.

CHAPTER XXVI.

SICKNESS AND DEATH.

CHAPTER XXVII.

MAN PROPOSES, GOD DISPOSES.

CHAPTER XXVIII.

CONCLUSION.

CHAPTER I.

SUTTON-POOL.

Where it is—Boys wading therein—John—A Short Tale of Poverty—The Five Points of Plymouth—John's Noble Spirit—Like Budgett and Bowditch—John only remembered of the Boys in Sutton-Pool—An Accident—His Paintings.

THE old town of Plymouth, England, contained a place, forty years ago, known by the name of Sutton-Pool. It was a harbor, or basin, into which trading vessels discharged their cargoes. At low water, it was converted into a mass of fetid mire, rendered still more disagreeable by being the receptacle of the town drainage, in which poor boys and girls were wont to wade, searching for bits of iron and rope, and such other things as might be washed or thrown therein. Notwithstanding the bad odor and filth of the place, fifty children were sometimes seen at once, wading up to their knees in the mire, well satisfied if they obtained a penny's worth of old iron in a day. Some of the most dexterous boys would make three-pence in a day, but only a few of them were thus successful.

Among the lads who waded in this Pool was one whose name was John — a bright, intelligent, active boy, some twelve or thirteen years of age. His home was like the homes of many children in large towns and cities — poor and comfortless. Perhaps the reader has seen the little "rag-pickers," "match-girls," and "street-sweepers," in a populous city. In New York there are thousands of this class, and other thousands who gain a wretched subsistence by still more menial ways. They are met in almost every street, shoeless, hatless, friendless wanderers, attracting the notice of strangers by their miserable plight. There is many a sad and touching tale that might be told of these penniless ones. The saddest and darkest portion of their lives were never written. Enough is known of them, however, to move the most unfeeling heart. The story of one of this class has been told as follows: —

"She lives in a rear building where full daylight never shines — in a cellar room where pure dry air is never breathed. A quick, gentle girl of twelve years, she speaks to the visitor as he enters — 'Mother does not see you, sir, because she 's blind!' The mother was an old woman of sixty-five or seventy years, with six or seven others seated around.

'But you told me you and your mother and little sister lived by yourselves.' 'Yes, sir — here it is;' and at the end of the passage the visitor discovers a narrow place, about five feet by three. The bed was rolled up in the corner, and nearly filled the room. 'But where is your stove?' 'We have none. The people in the next room are very kind to mother, and let her come in there to warm — because, you know, I get half the coal.' 'But where do you cook your food?' 'We never cook any, sir; it is already cooked. I go early in the morning to get coal and chips for the fire, and I must have two baskets of coal and wood to kindle with by noon. That 's mother's half. Then, when the people have eaten dinner, I go round to get the bits they leave. I can get two baskets of coal every day now; but when it gets cold, and we must have a great deal, it is hard for me to find any — there 's so many poor chaps to pick it. Sometimes the *ladies* speak cross to me, and shut the door hard at me, and sometimes the *gentlemen* slap me in the face, and kick my basket, and then I come home, and mother says not to cry, for may be I will do better to-morrow. Sometimes I get my basket almost full, and then put it by for to-morrow; and then, if next day we have enough, I take this to a poor woman next door. Sometimes I get only a few bits in my basket for all day, and may be the next day. And then I *fast,* because, you know, mother is sick and weakly, and can't be able to fast like me.'"

The "short and simple annals of the poor" furnish many sad tales like this. Nor are they confined to Cow Bay and The Five Points of New York. They are found in every large town and city. There was a Five Points in the old port of Plymouth, and "Johnny" dwelt upon its borders. He knew from bitter experience what poverty was. His home was uncheered by the many comforts which probably the reader enjoys at the fireside. No luxuries were there; indeed, there was often too little bread in the larder to satisfy the cravings of hunger. "Johnny" knew what it was to go to bed supperless — to walk the streets in tattered garments — to be cold and poorly clad — to be sick without the comforts that seem necessary — to look forward with no prospect of a brighter future — to look backward with nought but penury and friendlessness to recall of life's experience — to hope against hope — and to cherish many a secret wish for better days, which was all a wish. Poverty compelled him to hunt for broken-glass in the mud of Sutton-Pool. Every farthing he could get in this humble way, made his home happier, and lightened the heavy burdens of life.

John was not ashamed to earn a cent in any way that was honest. Many lads would not consent to assist themselves or parents in this humiliating manner. Their pride would not allow them to do this last of all work which the needy are compelled to undertake, or starve. These boys make that class of men, whose aristocratic notions lead them to despise some honorable pursuits, and to aspire to more popular vocations, where they fail, and cheat dependents often out of their just dues. John had no such pride. Perhaps the reader will say that he had nothing to be proud of. Well, perhaps he had not, unless it was his noble spirit. Nay, it was that very spirit which kept pride out of his heart, and made him willing to delve in "mud and mire" for an "honest cent." Had he been so indifferent to his parents and himself as to run the streets without caring whether he earned a cent or not, how much less manliness there would have been in his character! Boys of such a spirit usually become vicious in early life, and make vagabonds before they have lived out half their days. Samuel Budgett was laughed at by some people, both old and young, because he carried a bird or fowl through the streets offering it for sale; but he cared little for sneers and jests at his own expense, so long as he could honestly obtain a trifle thereby to aid his needy parents. His noble spirit raised him above the fear of such unjust ridicule. So, Nathaniel Bowditch, the great mathematician, wore his summer clothes to school one *winter*, because his parents were too poor to purchase warmer garments for him. His companions jested over his necessity, and poor "Nat," as he was called, had to endure insult heaped upon ridicule. But he bore it like a hero, willing to be the subject of derision, if he could only gratify his desire for knowledge. He could submit to wear the poorest garments of all the boys; but he would be second to no one of them in scholarship. Just this spirit was in the breast of our noble John of Plymouth. It was one of the ornaments of his childhood and youth. It helped lay the foundation of the excellent character he bore in after life, as we shall see in the sequel.

Of all the boys who were accustomed to wade in Sutton-Pool, John alone is known and remembered. It might seem strange indeed that even one of this poor class should establish a reputation for learning and excellence that would live long after he was dead. There is little in the appearance and condition of such a poverty-stricken group of children to promise a bright and honorable future. So many of this neglected class become vicious, and are known only in the annals of crime, that even one instance of superior excellence and success among their number is a marvel. The case of John is one of unusual interest. While the memory of other lads around Sutton-Pool has passed away, not one of them having lived so as to be recollected for his character or his home, the hero of this little volume is known in almost every land. A solitary representative of the poor district of Plymouth, as it was half a century ago, he lived to show that the brightest gems of intellect are sometimes picked from the rubbish of ignorance, and the fairest pearls of virtue from the sewers of iniquity.

An accident put a stop to Johnny's toils in Sutton-Pool. One day he trod upon a piece of glass concealed in the mire, and cut his foot badly. He was unable to walk about for several days. It was quite a trial for him, but, on the whole, he bore it bravely. His active mind could *think,* though he was confined to the house. It proved, in the end, a great blessing to him. For, it was while he was obliged to stay at home that his attention was directed to a juvenile enterprise which had somewhat to do with his love of learning some years afterward. It occurred to him that he might use the remnant of his box of water-colors, with which he had decorated all the pictures he could find hitherto, in preparing a set of original paintings, to sell when he might get able to go out. This was good work for his mind. Accordingly he set himself about the art of designing. Houses, trees, horses, birds, and some other objects were soon sketched and painted upon pieces of paper in the best style of the art among boys. True, the houses were not very well proportioned, and the trees invariably had the same form, while all the birds on their branches were as large as ostriches, some of them quite as large as the trees themselves. But John considered them good specimens of early artistic efforts, and when he put them up in the window for boys and girls to see, he was gratified to hear them pronounced "fine." Of course he thought these complimentary opinions proceeded from good judges, and they served to confirm his own views of the paintings produced.

For the present we shall leave Johnny and his

pictures, and recur to the still earlier years of his life. There are some incidents in his previous history, before he cut his foot in Sutton-Pool, which not only exhibit the character of the boy, but also foreshadow the future man. To these we turn for a moment.

CHAPTER II.

HIS GRANDMOTHER.

Cause of his Father's Poverty—A Drunkard's Home—Dr. Johnson's remark—Change at four years of age—His Grandmother—Excursions in the Fields—Kitto's Recollection of the Old Lady—The Merry Shoemaker—Stories of Cinderella and Blue Beard—Mrs. Barnicle's Shop—The Old Family Bible—Pilgrim's Progress and Gulliver's Travels—Present of a Box of Water Colors—Reading to his Grandmother out of the Bible—Imitates Dr. Hawker in a Chair-Pulpit—Stories of the Shoemaker and the Family Bible gave Direction to his Life—Picture of a Soldier made Wilkie a Painter—A Newspaper and Dictionary made Bloomfield a Scholar—Commenced Letter-Writing—A Valuable Exercise for the Young—A Scene for an Artist—Writing a Story with Illustrations—Juvenile "Theatricals."

WHEN John was born, on Dec. 4th, 1804, his father was in better circumstances than he was a few years afterwards. He had become addicted to the use of intoxicating drinks, and habits of intemperance were already formed. Nor was it a matter of much concern or remark at that time; for drunkenness was very prevalent. Ale-houses abounded in every village, and it was not regarded disgraceful to visit them. John's father was a frequent visitor at these abodes of ruin; and the result was that he became a confirmed drunkard.

It is a hard lot to be poor; but when poverty is entailed by intemperance, it is harder still. Little children, half-clad and half-fed, present a sad picture of humble life; but how much more touching is their misery, when a drunken father is the cause of their degradation! A home that is uncheered by ordinary comforts, where a devoted mother toils early and late to supply her little ones with bread, even in scanty allowance, is desolate enough. But when the demon of intemperance enters there, converting the husband and father into a brute, so that he often goes out and comes in with curses on his lips, it is too desolate to deserve the title, *home.* Yet such was Johnny's home.

Here, then, is the cause of that penury to which he was born. In this respect, his condition was not unlike that of thousands of children in our cities and country towns. Intemperance is the legitimate cause of three-fourths of all the poverty in this and other lands. It leads to idleness, which is the nursing mother of want. Dr. Johnson once said, "Drunkenness is the parent of idleness; for no man can apply himself to the business of his trade, either when he is drinking or when he is drunk. Part of his time is spent in jollity, and part in imbecility;

when he is among his companions, he is too gay to think of the consequences of neglecting his employment, and when he has overburdened his stomach with liquor, he is too feeble and too stupid to follow it. Poverty is the offspring of idleness, as idleness of drunkenness; the drunkard's work is little, and his expenses are great, and therefore he must soon see his 'family distressed, and his substance reduced to nothing.'" So it was with Kitto, the senior. His love of strong drink interfered with close attention to his trade, and finally beggared his family.

Intemperance appears to have been the curse of the Kitto family. For, not only the father of John, but his maternal grandfather, and his uncle, William Kitto, were drunkards. The former was a clever man, and his intemperance was periodical. One night he went from Plymouth to Bigbury, on horseback, a distance of thirteen miles, and there he became intoxicated. On his return, his horse trotted into a pond, and his rider fell off and was drowned. The latter was a man of superior education, but strong drink overpowered him, and he was reduced very low. Before he died he worked upon the Hoe as a pauper. It was a source of shame and grief to John Kitto, the boy, that his ancestors were thus intemperate; and he once concluded a long account of his uncle's career by saying, "Drunkenness is the bane of our family, and the name of Kitto is synonymous with drunkard."

John was relieved, however, in a measure, from the extreme sufferings of a miserable home, at four years of age. At that period, the family were in such straitened circumstances, that his grandmother Picken proposed to take him home with her. She was a kind, affectionate old lady, in humble circumstances, and cherished a most tender regard for little "Johnny," as she called him. In his new home he was cheerful and happy, and contributed not a little to make his grandmother so. Her attachment to him strengthened every day, until his presence became indispensable to her happiness. He sat with her much of the time, listening to exciting stories, and making patchwork. Unlike many boys of his age, he cared little for the amusements of lads in the street, and rather preferred his grandmother for a companion, and her stories of wizards and witches for a treat.

This good woman was aware that exercise, fresh air and sunshine, were necessary to promote such a boy's physical health, so that she occasionally rambled with him, cane in hand, in the green fields. They collected flowers, nuts, and other wild fruit, more particularly for "*Johnny's sake.*" These excursions were a source of great delight to our little hero, who fostered, in this way, a love for the beauties of nature, which he carried with him through life. They served, also, to endear the kind old lady to his heart. Perhaps no incidents of his life in his grandmother's humble abode, were remembered with more pleasure, in after life, than these rambles in the flowery lanes and fields. They were ever associated with the memory of the "dear old woman," as he was wont to call her in his manhood. Years after these juvenile explorations, he wrote of her as follows to a friend: —

"I cannot think of her without deep emotion, and if there were any one of the pleasant things which I once hoped for, and which are now impossible to me, that I would sooner than any other thing wish for again, it would be that she, of all my dead ones, should revive, or should still have lived, to exult, as she would have done more than any — more than I do myself — in my little triumphs over the unhappy circumstances in which she left me. But this can never be. I have lost the objects both of my passionate and passionless attachments, and now there is none so to exert that softening influence on my feelings, none so to rejoice in my successes, none so to sympathize with me in all that makes sorrowful or glad, as they would have done. I therefore feel as wanting a stimulus to exertion, which no circumstances can now supply to me, and which might have enabled me to effect more and better things than I can now hope to accomplish. No! my Andrew, I am poorer, much poorer in every respect, than you imagine."

There is little doubt that it was a happy thing for John that he was thus early brought under his grandmother's care. It took him away from influences at home that might have proved his ruin. It brought him into contact with another class of objects, and awakened new and fresh thoughts in his mind. Other facts to be narrated will show this quite as well as those already cited.

Near by his grandmother's dwelling, there lived a merry shoemaker by the name of Roberts. He was a great story-teller, and could whistle almost any tune known in the neighborhood. He was a clever, good-natured man, also, well suited to entertain the young. "Johnny" was permitted to visit Roberts at his shop, where he was both pleased and astonished with the thrilling tales he rehearsed about Blue Beard, Jack the Giant-killer, Cinderella, Beauty and the Beast, and others of a similar character. They were not very elevated stories, it is true; and they cannot be recommended for their tendency. But they were the first stories of a marvellous character to which the boy had listened, and they filled him with wonder. At the same time he was told that these tales were actually in print, and could be seen in Mrs. Barnicle's shop at the head of Market street. This intelligence awakened his curiosity, and henceforth he longed to become the possessor of these wonderful little books. Every half-penny that he got was carefully laid aside for the purchase of the coveted volumes. Within eighteen months he possessed as many of them as could be packed into a box seven inches long, four wide, and three deep. He was one of Mrs. Barnicle's best customers, so far as the number of books purchased was concerned. Their contents, too, he greedily devoured, and soon became as familiar with Cinderella, Blue Beard, and kindred tales, as the whistling shoemaker himself.

His fondness for reading, however, increased faster than his possession of books. He could neither buy nor borrow so many as he wanted to read. In his eagerness for them, he overhauled his grandmother's shelves, where he found a family Bible, a Prayer Book, Gulliver's Travels, and Bunyan's Pilgrim's Progress. The last two he read with the utmost delight. He could not let them alone till they were read through. Being illustrated volumes, he admired the engravings which they contained, and proceeded at once to make what he regarded an improvement upon the work of the artist, by coloring them with his grandmother's indigo, using a feather for a brush. His ingenuity, in this artistical way, was less conspicuous than that of Benjamin West at about the same age of life: for he made quite an ingenious brush out of the tip of the old cat's tail, with which he executed many pictures.

Some one who saw Johnny's embellishments of the "Pilgrim," and "Gulliver's Travels," presented him with a cheap box of water colors, with which he was of course delighted. Reading and painting now wholly occupied his time, and he lost what little relish for play he ever possessed. His grandmother was delighted with his studious habits, and, in order to gratify him, and keep him in the house, she borrowed such books as her neighbors had, so that for some time the little fellow found a plenty to do. But in process of time, he had read all the books which the street contained, and earned the reputation of being a "book-worm," which was very much in his favor.

The reader is perhaps anxious to learn what use he made of the old family Bible which he found upon the shelves. We will see. This sacred volume contained a large number of engravings, faithful representations of Bible scenes. These afforded him much pleasure, and gave him many new ideas of the Scriptures. He carefully read so much of the text as explained the engravings, though he was little interested in other portions of the volume. On Sunday, however, when Mrs. Pickens was unable to attend meeting, he was obliged to read a few chapters to her. The manner in which he performed this duty shows that he must have been a very close observer at church. For when he read the Bible to her, he always constructed a pulpit, by taking out the bottom of a chair and placing it before him for a cushion, while he occupied the enclosed space, to which he could now gain access. When he had fairly inaugurated himself minister *pro tem.*, he commenced reading, "as nearly as he could, in the voice, manner, and attitude of Dr. Hawker," the preacher to whom he was accustomed to listen. He had been so good a hearer in the sanctuary, and had observed the manners of Dr. H., so cleverly, that his imitation of him was somewhat striking. But it did not please the good old lady. She thought it amounted almost to profanation thus to play the minister; but she could not reason it out of "Johnny." He would read like Dr. Hawker, or he would not read at all. Like many other boys, he was sometimes obstinate, and his grandmother was too indulgent to insist upon obedience. So he triumphed, and read his own way.

These incidents are cited to show the origin of this boy's love of books. The shoemaker's stories, and the volumes found on Mrs. Picken's shelves, appear to have been the exciting cause of his desire for learning. The family Bible, whose pictorial illustrations afforded him unmingled pleasure, directed his thoughts more particularly to the narrative portions of the Scriptures. There appears to have been an intimate connection between his interest in that old copy of divine truth and his "DAILY BIBLE ILLUSTRATIONS," written thirty years thereafter, and now

4

known throughout Christendom. In his manhood, he was wont to refer to this incident of his childhood, as having directed his attention to that branch of Biblical literature in which he became so highly distinguished. It appeared to him that the circumstance of his finding that copy of the sacred record, and perusing it intently, had not a little to do with deciding his destiny. The sequel will make it appear still more like a provision of an All-wise Providence for that time when a direful misfortune closed the ordinary pursuits of life against him.

It often happens that some such event of early life exerts more influence than all things else in determining a person's career. The simple circumstance of seeing a colored drawing of a soldier, determined the course of David Wilkie, the celebrated artist. He once spoke of the fact as follows, in reply to a baronet, who asked him how he happened to become a painter: "The truth is, Sir John, that you made me a painter. When you were drawing up the statistical account of Scotland, my father had much correspondence with you respecting his parish, in the course of which you sent him a colored drawing of a soldier in the uniform of your Highland Fencible Regiment. I was so delighted with the sight that I was constantly drawing copies of it; and thus, insensibly I was transformed into a painter."

Robert Bloomfield, the poet, was left without a father at one year of age. His mother had five other children to support, with very small means at hand upon which to depend. When Robert was fifteen years of age, he went to London to learn the shoemaker's trade, of his two eldest brothers, who were working at that business. His mother had previously written to them to secure their assistance in supporting Robert. To this application George replied, that "if she would let Robert come to town, he would teach him to make shoes, and his brother Nathaniel would clothe him." This was a good opportunity, and accordingly Robert was sent to London, with the following charge to his elder brothers: "As you value a mother's blessing, watch over him, set good examples for him, and never forget that he has lost his father." He was received by his two brothers in a garret in Bell Alley, Coleman street, where they had two "turn-up" beds, with five workmen in all. It was not a very inviting place, as the following description of it by George, will show. "As we were all single men, lodgers at a shilling per week each, our beds were coarse, and all things far from being clean and snug, like what Robert had left at Sapiston. Robert was our man to fetch all things to hand. At noon he brought our dinners from the cook's shop; and any one of our fellow-workmen, that wanted to have any thing brought in, would send Robert, and assist in his work, and teach him as a recompense for his trouble. Every day when the boy from the public house came for the pewter pots, and to learn what porter was wanted, he always brought the yesterday's *newspaper*. The reading of this newspaper, we had been used to take by turns; but, after Robert came, he mostly read for us, because his time was of the least value." It was fortunate for him that his time was least valuable; for the reading of that paper was the beginning of his literary career. He frequently met with words which he could neither pronounce correctly, nor understand; so George, seeing a small worn English Dictionary in a book-stall one day, purchased it for four-pence. With this, Robert made rapid advancement in reading, and in a knowledge of the English language. The newspaper and Dictionary together served him a good purpose. They created in his heart a love of books, and started him off upon a course of thought and study in which he became distinguished.

As the drawing of a soldier in colors was the predisposing cause of Wilkie's choice of painting as a life-pursuit, and the newspaper and Dictionary of Bloomfield's career as scholar and poet; so the stories of the Plymouth cobbler and the pictorial family Bible exerted a determining influence upon the life of Kitto.

It was while living with his grandmother, that John made considerable progress in the art of writing composition. He was in the habit of borrowing books of his acquaintances, and his applications for them became so numerous that he began to feel somewhat diffident about asking for the loan of more. For the purpose of satisfying his modesty, and securing books at the same time, he resorted to writing for the volumes he desired. These letters abounded in apologies for his repeated calls, and were, in all respects, remarkable specimens of the artless simplicity and brightness of the boy.

This proved a valuable exercise to him. Letter-writing, is, perhaps, one of the best mental exercises in which the young can engage. It is an easy and profitable way of beginning to write composition, an art which is exceedingly valuable to a person in any calling in life. It forms the habit of thought, and cultivates an easy, graceful style of writing, which is always agreeable. It can be commenced, also, at a very early age, as soon as the letters of the alphabet can be made. This exercise cannot be urged too strongly upon the attention of the young. All can make more or less proficiency in the art by the time they attain to ten years of age. And it will contribute largely to refinement of manners, and the development of intellect.

Look again at this beautiful picture—the boy, Kitto, inspired with the desire for learning, yet too modest to express his thirst for knowledge in words, sitting down to utter in writing the longing of his mind for books! Too poor to buy, too noble to beg, too modest to borrow them, where he has repeatedly enjoyed similar favors, he strives to *write* the unquenchable earnestness of his soul for mental light, and becomes an humble suppliant at the feet of those who have enough and to spare! Unconscious of the intellectual powers within him, he asks for books to read as a pleasant pastime, but commences a career from that moment, almost unparalleled in the world of letters! It is a picture worthy of an artist's pencil. The triumphs of industry and perseverance might be forcibly illustrated by the faithful sketch.

That letter-writing led to other styles of composition, is evident from the following incidents. "A cousin, somewhat younger than himself, came to him one day with a penny in his hand, declaring his intention to buy a book with it. John was just then sadly in want of a penny to purchase the 'History of King Pippin,' (not Pepin,) so he asked his cousin whether he bought a book for the pictures or the story? 'Oh, the story to be sure!' John immediately offered to write him, for a penny, a larger and better story than he could get in print for the same money, and to clinch the bargain, said he would *paint* him a picture at the beginning, and he knew very well that there were no *painted* pictures in penny books. His cousin jumped at the liberal offer of author and artist in one, and sat down quietly on the stool to watch John's operations. When the double task was finished, John thought that he had well earned the penny, and, as, on reading the tale and viewing the 'pictorial embellishment,' his cousin was of the same opinion, no one else had a right to give a different verdict. Some years afterward, when John re-visited his native place, and was rather curious to get a sight at this tale, it was not to be found, and the only account his cousin could give of it was (and this was more than the author recollected,) that it was something about what was done in England at the time when wild men lived in it."

Another incident of John's early attachment to letters, is related in his own words, as follows: "My cousin, (the same referred to above,) his sister, another girl, and myself were one day together, when, having just read a play-bill, (as, indeed, I was in the habit of reading all the play-bills posted up in the streets,) it occurred to me that we should act a play. The idea was entered into with great glee; so, while they prepared dresses, I prepared play-bill and plot. The play-bill was soon done, and posted outside the street door. Of this, I remember only that the admission price was, to ladies eight pins, gentlemen ten. When we were all dressed, I instructed them in the leading ideas of the plot, leaving them to make the best of their respective characters, only suggesting what it would be best to say on some of the prominent occasions. When we entered in our various and grotesque attire, with paper caps and feathers, and others with old stockings on their heads, with ribbons, sashes, leather swords, and what-not, we found our audience to amount to fifteen girls and boys. As they were entertained and laughed plentifully at our tragedy, for a tragedy I think it was, as there was plenty of witchcraft in it, and only my female cousin remained alive at the end, no one had a right to complain. For the pins my aunt gave three half-pence, which we spent on apples and gingerbread. Of the feast thus supplied, when we had resumed our *lives* and usual attire, we invited our audience to partake."

These two incidents, particularly the first, show that the boy continued to advance in composition. The latter incident is cited for the literary bias it seems to indicate in the young author of the "play-bill" and "plot." At the time, he had never witnessed a play, nor even read one, and yet he promptly attended to the mental part of the amusement. It would not have been remarkable in a child who had ever seen a play; but in one who had not had the opportunity, it is evidence of decided attachment to literature. We would not be understood to recommend even such juvenile "theatricals" to the young. The scene is delineated in order to show that the first use of the pen at letter-writing, predisposed young Kitto to pursue the vocation of an author.

CHAPTER III.

A CHANGE.

Ten Years Old—Six Years Absence from Parents—His Father no better—The Ale-house—What his Mother did—His Way of getting time to Study—Wandering in Fields and sitting on Rocks—Pine Knots or "Pioneer Candles"—Unlike those who want things in a particular way, or none—The Author of "Newman's Concordance"—The Pioneer Preacher—The "Tip-Top" Study—Its Furniture, Bed, Chest, Two-legged Table, small Box, Paintings—Skeleton of a Dog's Head—His three Books—Recollection of this Study in after Life—St. Pierre wrote "Studies of Nature" in a Garret—Goldsmith in a wretched Lodging-Room—Kitto, like them—Becoming a Barber.

WHEN John Kitto was about ten years of age his grandmother's health became so much impaired, that he was compelled to become, in part, dependent upon his father. It occurred on this wise. An attack of paralysis totally unfitted his grandmother for house-keeping, so that she was obliged to relinquish it, and go and live with John's mother. Of course the boy went too. He had been six years absent from his parents, although he had enjoyed frequent opportunities of seeing them. The removal brought him under the supervision of both his parents and grandparent. The management of him was divided between the two parties. He had been so long the sole companion of his grandmother that the change was considerable; and yet, the habit of thought and study which he had formed was not interrupted by his removal.

John's home was no pleasanter when he returned to, than when he left it. It was rather more comfortless and wretched. For his father's intemperate habits had grown upon him, and his means of living were reduced in about the same proportion. He worked as journeyman mason wherever work could be found, excepting only those seasons when excessive drinking unfitted him for any work at all. His trade might have returned him ample means to support his family, but for his intemperance. Indeed, he earned enough in sober days to make his home comfortable and joyous, but the greater part of it was spent at the ale-house. He was frequently away at work in the country a whole week, and would stop at the ale-house as he returned on Saturday night, and there part with his last penny for drink. It was the lot of John to accompany his father in this job work, and he was often sent home alone on Saturday night, while his father tarried at some ale-house to revel till Sunday morning, and then go home moneyless to his family. Have many boys, at the age of ten years, so dark a prospect before them? Have many an experience so bitter, and a home so unattractive?

Mrs. Kitto was a woman of good resolution, or she would have sunk under her weight of trials. As the ale-house received most of her husband's earnings, she was obliged to support her family by her own exertions. At that time, it was difficult for a woman to find any definite employment whereby to gain even a scanty livelihood. Mrs. K. was sorely tried to find work sufficient to support her family. She was willing to perform any honorable service, if she could thereby secure bread for dependent ones. But here she met with great difficulty.

There was one thing, however, which she could do, especially when John was at home to see to the children. It was doing sundry chores for families around her. No opportunity of earning a half-penny in this humble way was unimproved, either by day or night.

But what time did John have for reading and writing? the reader will ask. The answer to this inquiry will reflect honor upon the boy, by showing how industriously and perseveringly he improved every leisure moment. His old practice of borrowing books of the friends he made (and he made them fast) continued. When his mother was at home, and his father did not require his assistance at mason-work, he would absent himself all day, and wander, with his book in his hand, through the fields, or sit "in the clefts of the rocks, till forced to make his escape from the tide, frequently by climbing up very precipitous and dangerous parts." He planned no time for play, none for idleness. Many lads of his age are continually studying how they can command the most time for sport. In school, their thoughts dwell upon the anticipated hours when they will be released from study. At work, they sigh for "nothing to do," when they can run and play to their heart's content. Not so with John Kitto. He wanted no time for play, no idle hours. If he could be alone with his book, it was the greatest privilege he could ask. Others might play; *he*, asked to read.

When John was left at home in the evening, in charge of the younger children, he managed to get them off to bed as early as possible, that he might have time to read and study. In this way he secured some precious hours for improvement. There was one obstacle, however, in the way of devoting his evenings to books, and such a one as few boys ever encounter. His mother was too poor to furnish him with lights for this worthy object. As he could not read in the dark, it became a matter of some interest, how light could be provided. "Necessity is the mother of invention," we are told, and it proved so here. He resolved to gather sticks enough in the day-time to burn in the evening, in the place of oil and candles that were wanting. This he did frequently; and his improvement continued about as marked as it would have done by the aid of the best of "sperm." Light he wanted, and it made very little difference to him how it was procured, if so be that his object was accomplished. There are many persons, both old and young, who must have wished-for blessings come in a certain way, or they cannot enjoy them. They are quite unable to adapt themselves to circumstances. They prefer to sit in the dark, mute and solitary, rather than to read by the blaze of a pine knot. It would make them nervous to light one of these "pioneer candles." They must have a lamp with the modern improvements, or they take very little comfort in doing anything whatever. They are troubled souls who are greatly to be pitied, since there is a poor prospect of their making a mark upon the world. In such times as these, when the road to distinction is open to those only who are already prepared for self-denials and vicissitudes, every person needs the spirit of John Kitto, who could study by the light of a blazing stick, when he could have nothing better. Such a spirit is noble and glorious, in comparison with that which must have things exactly so, or not have them at all. "If we can't do as we wish, let us do as we can," is an old and truthful saying—one that men who triumph over difficulties always reduce to practice.

This incident reminds us of one of a similar character in the life of a theological scholar of a former age; the celebrated author of "Newmen's Concordance." After this volume was published in England, he came to this country and settled in Rehoboth, Mass. He embraced the first opportunity to revise his valuable work, and re-publish it in a more complete form. He was not able to provide himself with "candles" for light during the long winter evenings, when he was obliged to prosecute this work; so he resorted to "pine knots" as the cheapest and only available way of lighting his study. Yet his ardor and perseverance were not a whit diminished; and his production was as valuable as if it had been prepared with the illumination of a splendid solar.

From the pen of Rev. W. H. Milburn, the blind clergyman, we have a sketch of the life of Dr. Bascom. He was a pioneer preacher of the West, and battled manfully with the difficulties and hardships of his circuit. His time for study was usually on the back of his horse, and in the cabins where he stopped for a night, or longer. The following extract will show with what readiness he adapted himself to circumstances, snatching from utter waste those fragments of time which he could, when stopping here and there for a night. "The cabin is twelve by fourteen feet, and one story high. The spaces between the logs are chinked, and then daubed with mud for plaster. The interior consists of one room, one end of which is occupied by a fire-place. In this one room are to sleep the man, his wife, the fifteen or twenty children bestowed upon them by Providence—for Providence is bountiful in this matter, upon the border—and as the woods are full of "varmints," hens and chickens must be brought in for safe keeping, and as the dogs constitute an important portion of every hunter's family, they also take pot-luck with the rest. Fastened to a tree near the door is a clapboard, upon which is traced, in characters of charcoal, a sentence to the following effect—which you may read if you are keen at deciphering hieroglyphics:—

"*Akomidations for man and Beast.*"

"In this one room the family are to perform their manifold household offices. Here their sleeping, cooking, eating, washing, preaching and hearing are to be performed. Amid the driving storms of winter, it is, of course, impossible for our youthful theologian to transform an old log, or the shadow of a tree into a study; his book must therefore be carried into the house, where he is surrounded by a motley group. Of course a hunter never swears in bad weather; the lady of the house never scolds; children of all ages never quarrel and raise a row; dogs never bark and fight; nevertheless, you may imagine that if our student is able to confine his attention to the page, deriving mental nutriment from the lettered line, he must possess not a little power of concentration and abstraction. He obtains permission of his host to pursue his studies after the rest of the family have retired. *Lighting a pine knot*, he sticks it up in one corner of the huge fire-place, lays himself down on the flat of his stomach in the ashes, glowing with transport over "the thoughts that breathe and words that burn."

Yet this same young preacher became a Doctor of Divinity, the President of a University, a distinguished Bishop in the church; and he always adorned the offices to which he was called. Had he belonged to that unyielding "notional" class, who cannot bring themselves down to enjoy a pine knot, he never would have been known out of the Western forest.

John Kitto had a better study than Henry Bascom. At the top of his father's tenement was a small apartment, seven feet long and four wide, which John was permitted to regard as his own. It might properly be called the "tip-top study." Here he could retire from the noise of the family when opportunity offered during the day, and at night he could pursue his studies there to a late hour. The thought of converting this into a study, did not occur to the lad until he had used the fields and the clefts of the rocks awhile for this purpose. But time brought a change. The garret soon presented quite another aspect. It contained a bed, very humble, indeed, but the best that could be afforded the young student. There was a little round table also, which was made by John's grandfather forty years before. As only two of the four legs it once possessed, remained, it required some little care to keep it in an upright position. But John probably thought that a table with two legs is better than none, and so congratulated himself upon having even so good a one as that. In addition to this furniture, there was an old chest in which he kept his clothes and stationery; also a small box constructed with his own hands, containing his water-colors, shells, and curious pebbles. Of this box, he said some years after, "a better satire on human security never existed. It was fastened with the great padlock of a stable-door, as heavy as the box itself, but attached to the box simply by pack-thread, so that a single stroke of a knife would have cut it off; its only use, therefore, was not to prevent pilfering, but to indicate that such an attempt had been made."

The walls of the room were ornamented with such prints as he had collected from time to time, together with a number of his own drawings. Over his bed was hung a singular and somewhat frightful object for one of his years to choose. It was the skeleton of a dog's head. He found it one day when he was strolling along the beach, and he carried it home with evident delight. As time and the waves had entirely removed the animal's eyes and tongue, he inserted artificial ones, and having colored the jaws with vermillion, in order to impart a fiercer look, he hung it up over his bed. What could have been his object in giving such prominence to the skeleton, or even in carrying it home from the beach, it is difficult to say. It was unlike almost any other expression of taste on his part. Possibly he might have chosen, and placed it there for the purpose of driving sleep from his eye-lids, as he awoke in the morning and beheld its hideous grin. It is quite certain, that its savage appearance was enough to make a nervous person wakeful.

In this room were found John's scanty, yet valuable library. It consisted of a very ancient Bible, printed during the reign of Queen Elizabeth, and a copy each, of Young's and Spencer's poetry. We make no mention of the various juvenile tales like Cinderella; for he had now advanced beyond a taste for these marvellous stories. If it be said that his library was *small*, it must also be conceded that it was *good*.

Often when Kitto was afterwards travelling in foreign parts, and when he was examining vast European libraries, his mind reverted to this period of his life. He loved to revisit the old garret in imagination, because it was so closely associated with his early struggles for knowledge. He said that those were his happiest days, because his young heart was satisfied with his means for intellectual improvement, however stinted, and neither trial nor misfortune overwhelmed his buoyant spirit.

Many eminent writers, at some period of life, have had a similar experience. St. Pierre, who was the author of the celebrated "Studies of Nature," speaking of the place where he labored upon this remarkable production, says: — "It was in a *little garret*, in the new street of Etienne Du Mont, where I resided four years in the midst of physical and domestic afflictions. But there I enjoyed the most exquisite pleasure of my life, amid profound solitude and an enchanting horizon; there I put the finishing hand to my 'Studies of Nature,' and there I published them."

Goldsmith had a similar experience. A friend visited him on one occasion, and found him in such a miserable plight in a poor lodging-room, that he said he should not have spoken of it, "had he not considered it the highest proof of the splendor of Goldsmith's genius and talents, that by the bare exertion of their powers, under every disadvantage of person and fortune, he could gradually emerge from such obscurity to the enjoyment of all the comforts and even the luxuries of life, and admission into the best societies of London."

It was in that humble abode that Goldsmith wrote his "Inquiry into the Present State of Polite Learning," and his "Vicar of Wakefield," two of the finest productions in the English language. There was but a single chair in the room; and when a visitor called, Goldsmith, with appropriate civility, offered him the solitary chair, and took a seat himself in the window.

If we should occupy time and space enough to record all, or even half the intellectual triumphs that have been made in stifled attics and wretched lodging-rooms, the most fastidious reader would cease to smile at John Kitto's humble beginning. The more lowly one's circumstances, the more glory in his triumphs. By this standard the subject of this volume will be tried, as we proceed with his remarkable history.

It may be added here, that about this time, John's father sent him to learn the barber's trade, that he might be able to earn something for his own support. He was rather young to undertake this work, being only eleven years of age; but an opportunity offered, and the intemperate father was glad enough to avail himself of it. The barber, to whose discipline he was subjected, is described as follows by John: — "Old Wigmore had practised on board a ship-of-war, and related adventures which rivalled Baron Munchausen; had a face so sour that it sickened one to look at it, and which was beside, all over red by drinking spirituous liquors."

He did not continue long in this employment, however. The following incident led to his dismissal. John was wont to take charge of his master's best razors, and carry them home with him at night. It was his business in the morning to open the shop. One morning, as he came to the shop, with the razors and other things in a bundle under his arm, he found a woman waiting at the door for Wigmore, as she said. John, ready to oblige her, acceded to her proposal, and ran to call his master, leaving his bundle in her charge at the door. When he returned no woman was there, and the razors, of course, were gone with her. Wigmore was angry, and dismissed the boy on suspicion of his being an accomplice with the thief. John was rejoiced to be delivered from the care of such a man, though he keenly felt the imputation of being called an assistant thief.

CHAPTER IV.

FEARFUL CALAMITY.

His Fall—Two Weeks of Unconsciousness—The Crisis Passed—Reason Restored—Call for a Book—William Mason—Archimedes—His sense of Hearing Destroyed—The Startling Announcement—A New World—His account of the accident in his "Lost Senses"—How he Accounts for the Misstep—A World without a Sound—A Dark Prospect.

WE have seen that John was in the habit of assisting his father at mason-work a portion of the time. It is true, the aid he could render was small, but very little helps a needy family. He could carry some bricks and slates, and certain other materials used in his father's business.

On the thirteenth day of February, 1817, he went with his father to a job in Batter street, Plymouth. The particular work which he had to do, was repairing the roof of a house, and John was employed in carrying slates thither. It was about half-past four o'clock in the afternoon, when he was ascending the ladder with a load of slates, and was in the act of stepping upon the roof, that his foot slipped, and he was precipitated from a height of thirty-five feet on a stone pavement below. It was a fearful fall; and it was quite remarkable that none of his limbs were fractured. He was taken up insensible and conveyed to his home. While he was borne along the street, attended by a crowd, he had a few moments of half consciousness, when he realized that something had befallen him; but he soon lapsed into unconsciousness, in which state he continued for two weeks. They were two weeks of deep solicitude with his friends. The extent of his injuries could not be determined while he lay insensible. Life seemed to be well nigh extinct. The chance of his recovery was small indeed.

Two weeks after his fall, he opened his eyes, one morning, when the sun was two or three hours high, and, supposing it was considerable past his usual time of rising, he made a vain attempt to get up. He found that he was unable to lift a limb from the bed. His strength was gone, and he was as helpless as an infant. At first he was greatly surprised, as he had had no intimation before of being an invalid. This utter prostration, in connection with the apparent silence of his friends in the room, soon convinced him that he was sick; and yet he was not able to detect the cause of his weakness. He noticed persons engaged in earnest conversation, but he could not hear a word they uttered; and he concluded that they were conversing in a low undertone, from a kind regard to his feeble state. His mistake, however, was soon exposed by being made acquainted with the fearful fact.

His first thoughts, on being restored to consciousness, were of books. He at once began to make inquiries concerning a book, which the town-crier's wife had lent him just before the accident. This circumstance shows what a strong hold upon knowledge his mind had taken. Instead of asking what was the matter, or how he came there, he inquired for a volume which he was reading at the time of the fall, and in which he had become deeply interested. This incident reminds us of one in the life of William Mason, author of the "Spiritual Treasury." He became so absorbed in the preparation of that volume, as to be forgetful of almost every thing else. A gentleman called upon him one day, on business, and, instead of taking his name and address, as he intended, he wrote the chapter and verse on which he was meditating. When the time for him to wait upon the gentleman arrived, he looked for the paper, and found upon it only "*Acts the second, verse the eighth.*" More similar still, is the anecdote of Archimedes, the distinguished mathematician of Syracuse. When his native city was besieged, and the invading foe had entered it, driving the affrighted inhabitants before them at the point of their bayonets, Archimedes was engaged in demonstrating a geometrical problem. He was so completely absorbed in the problem, that, when his study was entered by soldiers, and he was warned away with uplifted weapons, he continued his mathematical work, simply requesting, in a quiet manner, *that they might wait till he had completed the problem.*

John's mind appears to have commenced effort, after consciousness was restored, just where it was interrupted at the time of the accident. Although two weeks had elapsed, his mind seemed to awake to activity, as if it had slumbered but for a moment. That which was most upon his mind, at the time he was stricken down, was first in his thoughts when he was restored to conscious life. He asked for the borrowed book, but heard no response. Thinking that his request was unheeded, he became impatient, and repeated it with greater emphasis. Still he heard no answering voice. "Why do you not speak?" he exclaimed; "Pray, let me have the book!" His friends looked at each other, and then at the suffering boy, evidently perplexed. At length, one of them hastily took up a slate, and wrote upon it: "The book has been returned to its owner, at his special desire, and if it had not, you are too weak to be allowed the use of it." This appeared to satisfy him on this point; but it gave rise to another mystery. "Why should they *write*, and not *speak?*" To one, who had been accustomed to listen to the music of pleasant voices, this oppressive silence must have been strange indeed. For a moment, he pondered the mysterious fact, and then exclaimed again, "Why do you *write* to me? why not speak? Speak! speak!" The by-standers exchanged glances again; they saw that the fearful truth could no longer be withheld. One of them took the pencil and wrote, "You are *deaf.*"

The announcement was wholly unexpected, and it must have startled him like a sudden clap of thunder. When last he met his friends, he could hear the tones of love and affection; and when last he looked abroad upon the face of nature, his ear was keenly alive to every sound that echoed over the winter fields. But now, how changed! To him, the earth had become as silent as the grave. Henceforth the sounds of earthly joy and gladness ceased to him. The world of music was blotted out. The harp and lyre lost their charming notes, and every musical instrument was voiceless as the stones. The forests rang no more with the sweet songs of birds. Choral vespers, that floated on the breezes over hill and valley, died away forever. Accents of human kindness and the melting tones of love were hushed. Eternal silence reigned throughout creation, to the poor, deaf boy. To him, the earth was characterized by an awful, unutterable absence of every conceivable sound. Sad, bitter experience! Poverty had stinted his fare from the day of his birth; and now, this terrible calamity added the severest trial of all! If penury was an obstacle in the pathway of the aspiring boy, what must be said of deafness? To close this principal avenue of knowledge, what a blight it must have brought upon the hopes of the student, struggling against want and obscurity, to ascend the hill of science! If we find that John Kitto triumphed over this additional misfortune, and won a place for his name among the worthies of the past, it will be a more remarkable example of enthusiasm and perseverance.

Kitto himself, at forty years of age, wrote as follows of that memorable day, in his work, called "The Lost Senses": — "The circumstances of that day,— the last of twelve years of hearing, and the first of twenty-eight years of deafness, have left a more distinct impression upon my mind than those of any previous, or almost any subsequent day of my life. It was a day to be remembered. The last day on which any customary labor ceases,—the last day on which any customary privilege is enjoyed, — the last day on which we do the things we have done daily, are always marked days in the calendar of life; how much, therefore, must the mind not linger in the memories of a day which was the last of many blessed things, and in which one stroke of action and suffering, — one moment of time, wrought a greater change of condition, than any sudden loss of wealth or honors ever made in the state of man. Wealth may be recovered, and new honors won, or happiness may be secured without them; but there is no recovery, no adequate compensation, for such a loss as was on that day sustained. The wealth of sweet and pleasurable sounds, with which the Almighty has filled the world, — of sounds modulated by affection, sympathy, and earnestness, — can be appreciated only by one who has so long been thus poor indeed in the want of them, and who, for so many weary years, has sat in utter silence amid the busy hum of populous cities, the music of the woods and mountains, and, more than all, of the voices sweeter than music which are, in the winter season, heard around the domestic hearth."

He also accounts for his misstep, on the roof of the house from which he fell, in the following way: —

"Three things occupied my mind that day. One was, that the town-crier, who occupied part of the house in which we lived, had been, the previous evening, prevailed upon to entrust me with a book, for which I had long been worrying him, and with the contents of which I was most eager to become acquainted. I think it was 'Kirby's Wonderful Magazine;' and I now dwell, the rather upon this circumstance, as, with other facts of the same kind, it helps to satisfy me that I was a voracious reader, and that the calamity which befel me, did not create in me the literary appetite, but only threw me more entirely upon the resources which it offered.

"The other circumstance was, that my grandmother had finished, all but the buttons, a new smock-frock, which I had hoped to assume that very day, but which was faithfully promised for the morrow. As this was the first time that I should have worn that article of attire, the event was contemplated with something of that interest and solicitude with which the assumption of the *toga virilis* may be supposed to have been contemplated by the Roman youth.

"The last circumstance, and the one, perhaps, that had some effect upon what ensued, was this: In one of the apartments of the house at which we were at work, a young sailor, of whom I had some knowledge, had died, after a lingering illness, which had been attended with circumstances which the doctors could not well understand. It was, therefore, concluded that the body should be opened, to ascertain the cause of death. I knew this was to be done, but not the time appointed for the operation. But, on passing from the street into the yard, with a load of slates, which I was to take to the house-top, my attention was drawn to a stream of blood, or rather, I suppose, of bloody water, flowing through the gutter by which the passage-way was traversed. The idea that this was the blood of the dead youth, whom I had so lately seen alive, and that the doctors were then at work, cutting him up and groping at his inside, made me shudder, and gave what I should now call a shock to my nerves, although I was very innocent of all knowledge about nerves at that time. I cannot but think it was owing to this, that I lost much of the presence of mind and collectedness, so important to me at that moment; for, when I had ascended to the top of the ladder, and was in the critical act of stepping from it on to the roof, I lost my footing and fell backward, from a height of about thirty-five feet, on to the paved court below."

We have spoken of what followed, but it may be well to have it in Kitto's own words. He says: "Of what followed I know nothing; and as this is a record of my own sensations, I can here report nothing but that which I myself know. For one moment, indeed, I awoke from that death-like state, and then found that my father, attended by a crowd of people was bearing me homewards in his arms; but I had then no recollection of what had happened, and at once relapsed into a state of unconsciousness.

"In this state, I remained for a fortnight, as I afterwards learned. These days were a blank in my life; I could never bring any recollection to bear upon them; and when I awoke one morning to consciousness, it was as from a night of sleep. I saw that it was at least two hours later than my usual time of rising, and marvelled that I had been suffered to sleep so late. I attempted to spring up in bed, and was astonished to find that I could not even move. The utter prostration of my strength subdued all curiosity within me. I experienced no pain, but felt that I was weak; I saw that I was treated as an invalid, and acquiesced in my condition, though some time passed, more than the reader would imagine, before I could piece together my broken recollections so as to comprehend it."

Kitto was confined to his bed four months. It was eight months before his health was so far restored that he exhibited much of the strength and elasticity which characterised him before his fall. But he was now in quite another state, and another world opened before him—a world without a sound. Let the reader conceive, if possible, how different would be the earth on which we live, if every sound were henceforth to cease, and universal silence to reign. It would be another state of existence. Translation to another planet would scarcely introduce the subject into more different relations. Yet such was the world to John Kitto. He must begin life anew, as it were. The past was of great service to him, but he must plan and study how to use it, to brighten the future.

Look now, at this poor deaf boy, thirteen years of age, and say if his prospects for life are not discouraging! If a person had predicted that, notwithstanding the unpromising ciscumstances of his early youth, he would in time become a man of letters, that theological science would receive valuable contributions from his able pen, that literature would claim him as a chieftain in its field, that the church would value the productions of his pen as a large legacy of wealth, and a precious memorial of the man, and that his name would be as familiar as a household word in the christian families of almost every land, he would have been pronounced a wild dreamer, or an irresponsible lunatic. Yet all this, and more, as we shall see, was true of the unfortunate, but noble boy, John Kitto.

CHAPTER V.

PAINS BRING GAINS.

No longer Works with his Father—How earned Pennies—His Picture Gallery—The Fair, and his Paintings—His Painted "Signs" and "Labels"—The Peddling Excursion—His Description of the Second one—His love of good Spelling—Disadvantages of bad Spelling, with Illustrations—Evidence of keen Observation in Kitto—Little Things Valuable—A bad Speller not get credit for much Knowledge, though he may possess it—A Letter from a Pupil's Father.

WE now return to that period of his life, of which we spoke in the first chapter, when he waded, with other poor boys, in Sutton-Pool. His deafness unfitted him to labor with his father at mason-work, as well as for almost every other kind of business. The consequence was, that he was left to follow his own inclination, in a great measure.

His love of books continued undiminished; indeed, it appeared rather to increase as a natural consequence of being so far excluded from social intercourse. But now, that he was not in the way of earning any thing for the family, he had fewer pennies to lay out in juvenile books. At the same time, he had nearly exhausted the stock of volumes owned by his friends and neighbors, so that his mind was famishing for proper aliment.

At this point, he decided to search for bits of iron and other things, in Sutton-pool. Although he could earn but a trifle in this way, yet the smallest gains would serve him a good purpose in the acquisition of knowledge. He was well qualified also, to derive the greatest good from the smallest means. While he would have been grateful for a dollar's worth of knowledge, he cheerfully accepted a pennie's worth, when that was all he could possibly get. So he engaged in the menial work described, with as much zeal as any one of his poor companions.

The accident of cutting his foot, with a piece of glass, disabled him, as we remarked in another place, so that there was no prospect of his returning to this employment for some time. While he was confined to the house, he bestowed much of his time upon the art of painting. His design of forming a sort of picture-gallery in one of the windows opening into a court, for the purpose of getting pennies, was not wholly a failure. Occasionally a passer-by, amused at the somewhat novel exhibition, and willing to contribute a little to the young artist's funds, dropped in a half-penny. His average income, during several weeks, was about twopence-halfpenny. One week he received eightpence; but this was on an extraordinary occasion, of which the following account is given in his own words: —

"During the fair at Plymouth, it is customary for industrious girls to have a "standing," as it is called, in the streets, generally outside their own doors. This standing consists of a small table, over which a napkin is nailed against the wall, and to this the various articles, which appertain to a doll's wardrobe, are fastened with pins, and thus exposed for sale, while the table itself is spread with smart pincushions and other matters, which do not easily admit of being pinned to the napkin. Behind these standings the girls sit on stools, like so many little patients on monuments, waiting for customers. The idea occurred to me of having such a standing during the fair for the sale of my pictures. The time was short, and I labored hard to provide an adequate supply of goods for the occasion. I then carried my intention into effect. The innovation was startling, and drew a degree of attention to the stall and its master, which was in the highest degree annoying to myself personally. But I faced it out; and the result furnished me with a larger sum of money than I had ever before possessed, as the fruit of my own spontaneous exertions."

This was certainly a plan entirely original with young Kitto, whatever may be said of its wisdom. England had never had such an exhibition before, and perhaps she has not had a similar one since. None but an independent, resolute and persevering youth, would undertake such an enterprise. It requires these noble qualities to "face it out."

As Kitto was walking about the streets, he frequently observed "signs" and "labels," which were spelled incorrectly. For instance, in one window he saw a notice of "Logins for Singel Men;" and the penmanship was about on a par with the spelling. It occurred to him that good spelling would be more acceptable even to the ignorant, than the opposite; and that labels prepared in colored capitals would soon supercede the homlier ones in general use. Accordingly, he applied himself very diligently, for a few days, to the preparation of a parcel of these articles, with which he set out on a peddling excursion. It was new business to him, and youth of his quietness and modesty do not generally make good pedlars. He reached the shop where the above singular advertisement of "Logins" was exposed, but his courage failing him, he did not dare to enter. He walked up and down the street as many as ten times, but even then his heart was too faint, so he turned his steps homeward. On his way he reproached himself for such timidity, and, partly to punish himself for cowardice, he hurried into a shop where he saw a very bad notice in the window, and made known his errand. A fine old spectacled woman sat there darning stockings, and her gracious smile inspired Kitto with fresh courage. For a deaf boy, who had nearly lost his power of speech also, to make known his errand to a stranger, and perform a successful peddling operation, was no small matter. He placed the book in which he carried his labels, upon the counter, and proceeded to turn over the leaves under evident excitement. He soon came to the one which he wished to sell, and, pointing to the queer notice in the window, he said, "*This* for a penny."

Never did an Otis, or a Lawrence, wait with half so much anxiety the consummation of a bargain of thousands, as this youth waited for the good dame's response. A penny was as important to him as thousands are to many a speculator in the marts of trade. It was to test also, the marketable character of his wares. This was the first counter upon which they were laid for sale, and his spirit would rise or sink within him, according as they were accepted or rejected.

The good woman examined the label with some care, and then indicated to Kitto that the price was too much. "A halfpenny, then," he replied. To this, she responded something which Kitto could not understand, whereupon he put his fingers to his ears in a manner to indicate that he was deaf. This at once enlisted the sympathy of the woman, and she threw down a penny without delay, to the boy's no small gratification. As he was about leaving the shop, she called to him to wait a moment, and soon brought forward a cup of milk and piece of cake for his refreshment. Such kindness touched a tender spot in his heart, and he thanked the kind-hearted woman with much emotion.

Although he was quite successful in this peddling excursion, he had not sufficient courage to undertake but one more. From time to time, however, he disposed of a label to his neighbors, who probably made the purchase out of regard to the boy, rather than from a desire to possess the articles. These contrivances to increase his funds, verify the proverb, "No gains without pains."

The reader may be interested to have Kitto's account of his second peddling trip in his own words. It is as follows: —

"My aunt encouraged me to offer the labels for sale. . . . . . After all, I had courage to offer them only at three places. Hear the result of these attempts. My first was in James street, at a retail grocer's shop, where I saw two wretched scrawls in the window, and no person, but an old woman, reading a Bible. In I went, took off my hat, and laid two of mine similar to hers on the table. 'Will you please, ma'am, to give a halfpenny each for these?' She ceased reading, and asked me ever so many questions, to which I answered at random, 'Yes' or 'No;' at last I was so hard put to it, that I was constrained to say, 'I am deaf, ma'am,' pointing to my ears at the same time. She looked surprise and pity, and gave me a penny for the two. The next attempt was in a street, where I saw in a window, badly written, 'Children taught to read and work.' I passed and repassed several times, glancing my eye at the window, but I could discover nothing through it, for there were muslin curtains before it. I tapped at the door; a man dressed like a sailor, who sat near it, opened it; there were in the room, an elderly woman, and two others, younger, who seemed to be her daughters, all dressed in genteel mourning, and sewing, and two men who seemed *lovyers* of the young females. I produced my label, and asked a penny for it; the man who opened the door, handed it to one of the young women; she examined and approved it, and the man gave me a penny. I tried only one place more, where I saw, '*Rooms to leet, Enquair withing;*' I offered a spruce 'Rooms to Let,' and asked a halfpenny; the door was opened by a crabbed-faced old woman, who scarcely deigned to look at it, but pointing to the one already in the window, seemed to say, 'That will do very well.' I did not venture to go to any more places, but with the threepence I had obtained, bought half a quire of paper, and went home."

We ought to stop here and consider more particularly Kitto's observation of bad spelling. It is a mark of some scholarship in a young person, and augurs well for the future. Many youth hurry on to the study of Philosophy and Algebra before they can master half of the spelling book. They think that good spelling is a small consideration in comparison with those higher branches of knowledge pursued in High Schools and Academies. It is the latter, they think, which embellish character, and not so unimportant a matter as spelling "Lodgings" and "Single" correctly. This class would have passed through the same streets with Kitto, without noticing anything peculiar in the "signs" and "labels" in the windows. Indeed, this was true of a large portion of the youth, of Plymouth, in his day. Perhaps not one in ten of them ever stopped to decide whether the spelling they saw was good or bad.

Now, we wish to impress upon the reader's mind the fact, that attention to such a small matter (small to the view of some) as correct spelling, is a more favorable omen than attention to many things usually regarded of far more consequence. That Kitto should particularly notice incorrect labels, tells more in his favor, at least, in one particular, than attention to the motions of the heavenly bodies would have done. Observation of *little things* sustains an important relation to character and future distinction. If these are properly regarded, the more important things of life wlll be sure to receive attention. He who is observant of minor affairs will not be likely to suffer superior subjects to pass unnoticed.

Moreover, this matter of spelling can scarcely be regarded a trifling thing. It lies at the foundation of a good education. It is one of the fundamental things in mental culture. If a man can be but one, a good speller or a good linguist, the former will serve him a much better purpose than the latter, and will often contribute more to his reputation. If his letters, and other written documents, are characterized by incorrrect spelling, it will leave a very unfavorable impression of his literary character upon the minds of others. For example, what is the general inference concerning the intellectual attainments of one who writes such a letter as the following? It was addressed to the author of this volume by a man whom he married. He was a stranger from a city, who appeared well, and was expensively dressed, but his letter caused another inference to be drawn, quite adverse to his literary attainments.

"Mr. Thare: You will confur a favor by sendin to me a certifikit of our marrige. It is customery for ministers in this city to give certifikits to parties whom they marry. It may be of servis to us at some future time.

"Yours Truly ———."

This man might have been well acquainted with Philosophy and Chemistry, but to the spelling-book he was somewhat of a stranger. It is doubtful, however, if he ever had credit with his correspondents for much proficiency in any branch of science. This deficiency in the trifling matter of spelling, as some youth are disposed to regard it, probably destroyed whatever claim he might have possessed to credit for advancement in the higher branches of knowledge. This was certainly the effect upon our own mind.

The following incidents, from the Massachusetts Teacher, will illustrate the subject further:—

"Some years ago, a teacher presented himself as a candidate for the mastership of a school, of which the salary was fifteen hundred dollars. His qualifications were deemed satisfactory in all respects, except in *spelling*. On account of this deficiency he was rejected. See, now, what ignorance in this elementary branch cost him. In ten years his salary would have amounted to fifteen thousand dollars, throwing out of the calculation the increase which, by good investment might have accrued from interest. Besides, the salary of the same school has since been advanced to two thousand dollars. But he might have remained in the position twice or three times ten years, as other teachers in the same place have done, and that large amount might, consequently, have been increased in proportion.

"A gentleman of excellent reputatation as a scholar was proposed to fill a professorship in one of our New England colleges, not many years since; but in his correspondence, so much bad spelling was found, that his name was dropped, and an honorable position was lost by him. The corporation of the college concluded that, however, high his qualfications as a professor might be in general literature, the orthography of his correspondence would not add much to the reputation of the institution.

"A prominent manufacturer, in a neighboring town, received a business letter from an individual who had contracted to supply him with a large quantity of stock; but so badly was it spelled, and so illegible the penmanship, that the receiver found it nearly impossible to decipher the meaning. An immediate decision must be given in reply; and yet so obscure was the expression that it was impossible to determine what should be the answer. Delay would be sure to bring loss; a wrong decision would lead to a still more serious result. Perplexed with uncertainty, throwing down the letter, he declared that this should be the last business transaction between him and the writer of such an illiterate communication; for, said he, 'I am liable to lose more in this trade alone, than I can make in a life-time of business with him.'

"A gentleman who had been a book-keeper some years, offered himself as a candidate for the office of secretary to an insurance company. Although a man of estimable character, possessed of many excellent qualifications, he failed of being elected because he was in the habit of leaving words misspelled on his books. The position would require him to attend to a portion of the correspondence of the office, and it was thought that incorrect spelling would not *insure* the company a very excellent reputation from their method of doing business, whatever amount might be transacted."

Inability to spell correctly exposes one to pecuniary loss. It is, moreover, an obstacle to an advancement to honorable station. Such instances as those cited above are satisfactory proofs; but that this defect in one's education is productive of mortification and mischief, is illustrated by the following actual occurrence.

A young teacher had received assistance from a

friend in obtaining a school, and wrote a letter overflowing with gratitude to his benefactor, but closed it thus: "Please *except* (accept?) my thanks for your kind favors in my behalf."

We have cited these incidents to show that bad spelling, which attracted the attention of Kitto, is an important matter to be considered by every youth. Hereafter they will be called upon to discharge public duties, and especially to write epistles, when defects of this character cannot be concealed. Some attention to the subject now may save them much mortification and many regrets hereafter.

CHAPTER VI.

A STEP HIGHER.

His Mind Wanted Stronger Meat—Three Penny Books—His First Shilling—The Book Peddler—The Sequel—His Integrity in the Matter—Uprightness brings its own Reward—Case of a Truthful Boy—Nicholas Biddle's Clerk—The "Youngster," Song of, by Cowper—Mrs. Bulley's Circulating Library—Kitto's Account of it—Expensiveness and Scarcity of Books in his day, an obstacle—The Change.

THE mind of John Kitto could not long be satisfied with such books as pennies and halfpennies would purchase. It needed more substantial nutriment as it gradually became developed.

How could he procure books of a higher price? This question occupied his thoughts for a time, and caused him some uneasiness. He had borrowed a few books of the kind his mind now craved; but he knew not where to borrow more. He had exhausted the supply of his acquaintances and friends, in addition to those penny and halfpenny volumes which he had been able to purchase. How could he obtain means to buy more valuable books?

He was content to advance one step at a time.

He knew that he must creep before he could go alone; and this is what many youth of his age have to learn. They scarcely know how to submit to the delay and toil necessary to fit them for higher stations. They would mount at once to the pinnacle of earthly prosperity.

The book-market furnished in his day, closely printed abstracts of popular fictions, and tales founded on Shakespeare, and other dramatic writers. These were published in the form of tracts, and sold for three cents each. Kitto could not think of purchasing works of higher value than these. Indeed, most youth, in like circumstances, would think they must use their pennies to protect themselves from cold and hunger. But Kitto's body could endure these evils with less misery, than his mind experienced in being denied appropriate nourishment.

He now aspired to purchase these three cent works. The first three-pence he possessed thereafter, was laid out in the purchase of one of these volumes. Nor did he delay at all in investing his money thus; but, fearing lest the pressure of external want might drive him to some other use of his pennies, he hastened to procure the coveted book. The reader may think that the selection of a book, under these circumstances, must have been perplexing to Kitto. It was not so; for long before he had the requisite means to purchase a volume, he had determined what one to take. He frequently visited the book-shop, for the purpose of examining the stock; and during some of these visits he decided what work he could add next to his possessions.

It was rather aggravating to Kitto to see so much literature of a higher and more desirable character, without being able to purchase it. Nor will a mind like his be long satisfied with that which is below its level. It will aspire to higher themes.

Kitto had laid by a shilling; the largest sum of money he had ever possessed. Soon after he became the owner of so much, a book pedlar called, with quite a variety of works, such as The Arabian Nights, Robinson Crusoe, Hervey's Meditations, Pamela or Virtue Rewarded, Pilgrim's Progress, and the History of Henry, Earl of Moreland. These were published in numbers, at a shilling each. He was particularly desirous of possessing a History of the French Revolution, which was decorated with a portrait of the Emperor Alexander, but his limited means would not admit the purchase. The pedlar, who was a close observer, soon understood the embarrassed condition of his young customer, and he proposed, that the work be taken fortnightly, instead of weekly. As Kitto had a shilling on hand, this proposition was at once accepted, and he took the first number with almost inexpressible pleasure.

The sequel proved that his calculation was some what at fault; for a shilling every other week, was more than he could possibly command. Before the fortnight had elapsed, he saw clearly, that he would not be able to meet his engagement. He was heartily sorry, that he had obligated himself to take the numbers, and he almost wished, that the book agent might forget to call. Moreover, he was not so much interested in the work, as he expected to be. It was rather dry, for even an intelligent boy of his years to read. This fact increased his disappointment, and how he should meet the agent honorably, he could scarcely tell.

At length Kitto resolved to prepare a plain written statement, to submit to the book-vender when he came. His resolution was carried into effect, and the document was ready by the time the man called. The paper contained an honest statement of the case, without any attempt to excuse himself on other than the real grounds. This incident is important, as illustrating the integrity of the boy. Some youth would have eluded the man if possible, or invented apologies for the occasion, or compromised the truth in some other way, in order to smooth the matter. But Kitto resolved to meet the case manfully, believing that a reasonable person, understanding the facts, would accept his apology. In this, he was not mistaken. For the vender of books, after reading the paper, justified Kitto, and offered to take the number back, at two-thirds of the original price, and release him from all further engagements. This was generous indeed. It was more than Kitto expected, and the kindness and pleasant manners of the man made a permanent impression upon his mind. Afterwards, he occasionally met him in the street, and always received a smile and sign of recognition from him.

In this instance, we see that uprightness brought its own reward. It was better for both parties, that the lad was conscientious in setting forth his inability to meet his engagement. The truth compelled him to acknowledge his extreme poverty, and this he did not hesitate to do. Many, both old and young, are ashamed to admit their penury, and even resort to modes of living beyond their means in order to conceal their want. But Kitto would confess all that the truth required; and his plain statement of facts pleased the bookseller, and won his esteem. There is little doubt that he was more favorable to the lad, on account of his truthfulness. Such exhibitions of youthful integrity, always leave a good impression upon beholders. They invest the young with a sort of nobility, which is highly honorable

The following is a similar example: — A lad was standing at the door of a neighbor, when a mother was calling after her little child, who was running away from her. Other ladies near by directed the lad in question, to run after him. He obeyed, and endeavored to bring back the child by force, but his struggles prevented. "Tell him," said one of the females, "that you have something for him, if he will return." "I shan't tell him so," responded the boy, "for I haven't any thing for him. That would be telling a lie." Did not those ladies think more highly of the boy, after this expressed regard for the truth? It would be strange if they did not. They might have felt rebuked for their unwise counsel to the lad, but his demeanor must have elevated his character very much in their estimation.

When Nicholas Biddle, Esq., was President of the United States Bank, he was applied to by the Directors of another bank to furnish them with a reliable young man, for cashier. Mr. B. at once named a clerk, who had been dismissed from the U. S. Bank, because he would not violate his conscience by writing on the Sabbath. He knew that a young man, who was so conscientious, could be depended upon in the important office of cashier. The independent stand he made for truth, became the cause of his promotion. At first, it cost him his place; but, at length, it brought him another, and a better one.

Many youth are like the "youngster," of whom Cowper sings, in the following poem: —

"A youngster at school, more sedate than the rest,
Had once his integrity put to the test: —
His comrades had plotted an orchard to rob,
And asked him to go and assist in the job.

"He was very much shocked, and answered, 'Oh, no!
What, rob our poor neighbor! I pray you, don't go;
Besides, the man 's poor, and his orchard 's his bread;
Then think of the children, for they must be fed.'

"'You speak very fine, and you look very grave,
But apples we want, and the apples we 'll have;

If you will go with us, we 'll give you a share,
If not, you shall have neither apple nor pear.'

"They spoke, and Tom pondered—'I see they will go;
Poor man! what a pity to injure him so!
Poor man! I would save him his fruit if I could,
But my staying behind, will do him no good.

"'If this matter depended alone upon me,
His apples might hang, till they dropped from the tree;
But since they *will* take them, I think I 'll go too,
He will lose none by me, though I do get a few.'

"His scruples thus silenced, Tom felt more at ease,
And went with his comrades the apples to seize;
He blamed and protested, but joined in the plan;
He shared in the plunder, but pitied the man.

"Conscience slumbered awhile, but soon woke in his breast,
And in language severe, the delinquent addressed:—
'With such empty and selfish pretences away!
By your *actions*, you 're judged, be your speech what it may.'"

John Kitto's integrity was made of sterner stuff. That undisguised sincerity and conscientiousness which characterized his dealings with the vender of books, would not yield to ordinary temptation. It was not only an ornament to his character, but it was a safeguard amid the moral perils around him.

Another incident, a few years later in Kitto's life,

is proof of his unyielding integrity. His father wanted to ask a favor of an officer at the poor-house (Mr. Barnard) where John then was; so he wrote upon a slip of paper, "Sir, I should be much obliged to you if you will be so good as to give a ticket for a shirt, as I am out of work—Jn. Kitto;" and desired his son to deliver it to Mr. B. John looked at it, and hesitated. "Father," at length he said, "thou sayest the thing that is not—you are not out of work." "You *must* give this paper to Mr. Barnard," responded his father. "Are you out of work, father?" asked John. "No!" was the emphatic reply. "Then do you think I will deceive my benefactor, and permit you to say through me, that you are? *I will not give it to him.*" This was John's noble decision. He would not lie, even for his father. He was the boy to carry a proper message for his parents, since he was obedient; but he could not carry a falsehood and satisfy his consceince. He knew that lying was a great sin in the sight of God, and he resolved that duty to his parents should not interfere with duty to his God.

A source of gratification was found by this young reader in a circulating library in Plymouth, owned by one Mrs. Bulley. Kitto availed himself of it so far as his pecuniary means would allow, although he was not pleased with the light character of the books. His hungry mind would devour unprofitable literature when it could not be provided with more substantial food. Some years afterwards, he referred to this library in the following language:—"These were works that afforded me amusement indeed, but from which I could not be expected to draw much instruction or information, at least, such information as I wished to obtain. Interested as I am, most deeply, in the welfare and improvement of that great body of which I am myself but a particle, and to whose service I desire to consecrate my best exertions, I exult beyond measure in the change which has taken place for the better, within my own time, and in the other and greater changes which I see before me; none but they who have known something of such struggles and difficulties as I have described, can well imagine the strong emotion which I sometimes experience as I view the windows of the numerous shops, which, in the various cheap publications of the day, do now, and ever must henceforth, offer advantages, the want of which formed so serious an obstacle to my own progress in the early part of my career."

In the above extract, Kitto alludes to an obstacle to the acquisition of knowledge which existed in his youth, to which the young of the present day are particularly strangers. The expensiveness of books rendered it well nigh impossible for the poorer classes to obtain many of them. A change in this respect, has been wrought in the last half century. Perhaps in no country has the change been more remarkable than it is in our own. Books, and other sources of information, are now brought within the reach of nearly every person. Their cheapness is not less remarkable than their numbers. Scarcely one generation ago, the juvenile literature of the land consisted of a few such books as Cinderella and Jack the Giant Killer. Very little attention was given to this class of books. Now, there are twenty millions of volumes in the Sabbath School Libraries of this country and Europe. Ten millions of them are found in this country alone. Juvenile papers, also, have become a source of much information. Not less than one million copies of these papers are circulated every month, in the Sabbath Schools of the United States. Hundreds of presses are constantly employed in printing them, and thousands of people in binding and spreading them far and near. Books for other classes have multiplied in about the same proportion. Of the making of many books, there is no end. They are too numerous to be numbered, and too various to be described.

CHAPTER VII.

THE POOR-HOUSE.

Worse and Worse—Removed to the Poor-House—Artifice used to convey him thither—The sad change described—Lowliest Home preferred to the Poor-House—The Governor's Kindness—His Good Behavior gained privileges—The Governor's successor—Kitto attends to Shoemaking—Does all things well—The testimony of eminent men.

WHEN Kitto was fourteen years of age, his grandmother removed from Plymouth to Brixton, while he remained behind, solely dependent upon his parents. This change subjected him to greater trlals than he had experienced before, and the year following was one of severe hardships. He was often compelled to go out in the cold, without half apparel enough to protect his body, and as often without sufficient food to satisfy the cravings of hunger. It was a hard, bitter lot, for one of his years to inherit, but there was no alternative. Strong drink continued to rob his home of comfort and joy, and the hand of poverty pressed harder and harder, upon his youthful head.

For a whole year he continued in this forlorn

experience. As the prospect of better days was still dark, and he was unable to follow any definite pursuit, on account of his deafness, he was sent to the Poor-House. This was in November, 1819, when he had nearly completed his fifteenth year.

It was supposed that Kitto would object to entering the Poor-House, where his liberty would be somewhat circumscribed. He had so long enjoyed even a larger liberty than other boys, on account of his inability to labor like them, that he would probably shrink from the restraints of such an institution. Consequently, his friends resolved to employ some artifice in removing him thither. Knowledge of the removal was studiously kept from him; and he was within the walls of the Poor-House before he became aware of their intentions. The first knowledge of the fact was almost overwhelming to him. His anguish was intense. He could endure poverty without shedding a tear; but to become an inmate of the pauper's home, was more than he could bear. He resolved to get away. He laid his plans for escaping, but they were never executed. In a little time he became somewhat reconciled to his condition, and was often happy in his new relations.

It is not surprising that he was thus excited and

grieved to find himself in a Poor-House. What boy would not be distressed to find himself some day, suddenly and unexpectedly transferred from his home to the alms-house! Even though his home were ever so lowly, it is nevertheless his home, where loved friends abide, and affection hallows every scene and object.

"'Mid pleasures and palaces tho' we may roam,
Be it ever so humble, there 's no place like home."

These lines of the poet awaken a response in the heart of every son and daughter who has enjoyed a home. Experience declares them to be the true language of the soul. If, then, a palace has less charms for man than the humblest home, how sad the change from such an one to the Poor-House! Amid the pleasures of a palace, where wealth is lavish of adornment and luxuries, the mind may find some bewitching objects of contemplation, but in the pauper's abode, there is naught to divert the thoughts from the home-scenes of better days. The inmates have only a tale of poverty to relate. Once they may have shared the smiles of fortune, but strange vicissitudes have dashed their fondest hopes. Dark shadows have fallen upon their paths, once irradiated perhaps, with the light of joy. The rooms they occupy are not devoid of comforts; and yet they seem to speak of penury. The furniture wears a forsaken aspect; and the very walls proclaim the poor man's fate. There is not an inch of soil around this pauper's habitation, unconsecrated to human want. It was bought by public charity in behalf of want. It is tilled for want. For want, its fallow ground is turned. Every seed is planted in its soil, and matured, after its upspringing, for want. Each blade of grass, and every vine and tree, grow and yield, out of mercy to pleading want. Thus, a Poor-House becomes itself, a living tale of woe. "That is a Poor-House," is a sad announcement to the passing stranger. The institution is associated in his mind with human privation and suffering. However pleasant its location, or beautiful its structure, it is still the abode of pauperism, and can never appear attractive. There is one class of emotions and associations that are always awakened by the sight of this abode, and they are of a melancholly cast. It has always been so. Perhaps it will continue to be so.

Was it strange, then, that the intelligent and aspiring youth, Kitto, was saddened and almost shocked, at finding himself a pauper in the alms-house of Plymouth ?

It was not long, however, before his mind became reconciled, in a measure, to his condition. The marked kindness of the governor, Mr. Roberts, served to hasten this result. His sympathy was enlisted by becoming acquainted with the boy's unfortunate condition, as the latter made it known to him in writing. He saw much in Kitto to admire, and the lapse of time increased, rather than diminished, his admiration.

The good behavior of Kitto, and his thirst for knowledge, in connection with his extreme want, so wrought upon the heart of Mr. Roberts, that he soon granted him a most precious privilege. It was to spend a day frequently at home with his mother. He was so grateful for this favor, and demeaned himself so well in improving it, that he was afterwards allowed to sleep at home nights, in that little upper room, or study, which we have described. Here he availed himself of the time at his disposal, for mental cultivation. He read all the books he could beg or borrow. Sometimes he sat up all night to read, though it was with difficulty that he could procure lights. At this time, he saved the pennies which were occasionally given to him, for the purpose of providing himself with candles. In this way he managed to turn the darkness of night into light, in order to gratify his thirst for knowledge.

Mr. Roberts did not long continue governor of the institution. It was a sad day to young Kitto, when he vacated his office; and he did not expect to find so true a friend in Mr. R.'s successor. But in this he was disappointed. For Mr. Barnard treated him with similar kindness, and their acquaintance ripened into a life-long friendship. This gentleman became one of his early patrons, and still survives to witness the proud achievements of the once deaf pauper. He is almost the only surviving one of his early friends, who aided him in his struggles after knowledge.

The reader may ask, if Kitto did no work while he was in the alms-house. We reply, that the rules of the institution required him to labor to a certain extent. He was accordingly placed under the care of Mr. Anderson, to learn the art of making list shoes. It was thought that he would be more successful in this branch of manual labor than in any other ; and he did make very commendable progress, so that he was subsequently bound to a shoemaker as an apprentice—a chapter of his life which will receive particular attention in another place.

It may be remarked, in this place, that whatever Kitto undertook, *he did well.* It appears to have been a trait of his character, to apply himself closely to whatever work he was required to perform. Hence his progress in making shoes. Subsequently, several of the first gentlemen of Plymouth interested themselves in raising funds for his education, and in the document they issued for this object, they spoke as follows of this talent in the shoemaking line:—"He has of late been employed as a shoemaker, in the work-house, and in that capacity he has given proofs of great skill and industry; but it seems desirable that he should be placed in a situation more consistent with his feelings and abilities, and to which his deafness might not render him incompetent."

CHAPTER VIII.

KEEPING A JOURNAL.

Kitto commences a Journal in the Poor-House—His reasons for so doing—Keeping a Journal beneficial—Hon. Robert Rantoul, Jr., and a record of his, at eight years of age—A record of one's actions useful—Pleasure in reviewing such a Journal—Extracts from Kitto's—The Soldier's Tear—Napoleon Bonaparte—Poetry.

IN August, 1820, Kitto commenced a Journal, which he continued until January 14, 1822, about a year and a half. There is much to learn of his character, and progress in knowledge, from the daily records in this interesting volume. His reasons for keeping this journal, he gave as follows, in November following the first record: —

"You have often asked me my motive for writing this Journal. It is this: — Finding in the leave Mr. Barnard had given me, I should want more books to occupy me than I could afford to get, and I did not like to take my drawing in hand unless I had time enough before me, and that when I had made the pictures I could not sell them, I resolved that, as writing is a good substitute for either, and more useful than the latter — I say, I resolve would write. What should I write? What, but a journal of my own actions! It is by far the most useful; for, as years on years roll on, and age shall — if I live so long — have numbered the powers of memory with those years, the journal will increase, and enable me *then* to look back on every prominent, and many of the minute features of my life, which hitherto have been marked by little but misfortune. And I doubt not that little of joy and much of sorrow will mark the remainder. I do not say, but that perhaps there was a bit of vanity in the resolution; but it is a harmless vanity to be able to produce, some years hence, a book of *my own* writing, and read some of it to my connections, to whom it will be indisputably interesting, as it concerns some of them."

Whoever heard before of a pauper keeping a journal? What a singular affair it must be! Surely, he must be a singular tenant of a poor-house who conceives such an undertaking. Some would say, "the boy must be crazy." What! A journal by a pauper, and he a deaf boy, too! But such is the fact, and it is an item worthy of consideration.

There is no doubt that the keeping of this journal exerted a happy influence upon Kitto, by aiding to develop his mental faculties. It is an excellent practice for one to adopt, even as early as ten years of age. It not only cultivates a talent for composition, but it fosters the habit of close observation, which is quite important in every sphere of human effort.

The late Hon. Robert Rantoul, Jr., commenced a journal at eight years of age, and continued it through the greater part of his life. He always highly valued the influence of this daily record upon his mental powers, and referred to it as among the causes of his elevation. One record, which he made at nine years of age, has often been quoted as indicative of his distinguished career. It is as follows :—

"Jan. 4, 1814.—Gained the following idea, namely; that I better sometimes be imposed upon than never to trust."

It was truly a bright idea for one so young to acquire, and it serves to show that children sometimes have thoughts that are worthy of an enduring record. But it was with reference to the benefit of journalizing, that we referred to this fact. Mr. Rantoul considered the influence of the practice so excellent upon himself, that he strongly recommended it to the young generally.

The three advantages of a journal, which Kitto mentions in the above extract, will usually be realized. They are, (1) mental improvement, (2) moral culture, (3) and future pleasure. He does not give these reasons in so many words, but they are the real reasons contained in his record. In respect to the first, no one can cherish the least doubt. The second refers to a record of his own actions. It must be morally beneficial for any person to keep a faithful account of his daily actions, good, bad, and indifferent. The review of them, thus recorded, must serve to check unbridled passions, and lead to the cultivation of the sterner virtues. Virtues and vices appear in their true colors, more attractive and repulsive than the journalist had expected. As to the third, future pleasures, it appears evident, that it must be a source of pleasure, in after life, to run the eye over the details of youthful days, as recorded, at the time. On this point, we have the testimony of many individuals who speak from experience.

Let the reader of this volume prove the truth of these remarks, by keeping a journal, without delay. Let it contain, not only an account of important events that occur in the world at large, but especially a somewhat minute detail of his own actions, plans, and achievements. It will be a useful volume to him, many years hence, if he survives; and, if he dies, it will be a precious legacy to friends, that linger awhile behind.

In order to exhibit Kitto's progress in composition, we make the following extracts from his journal. Let it be borne in mind, that he was only sixteen years of age, when he penned them.

One day he was passing along the streets, when he witnessed a touching scene which he thus describes:—

"Oh, for thy pen, pathetic Sterne! thine, too, Mackenzie! to relate as follows. No, not thy pen, bootless gift; thy pen were not better than another's. In thy brain, and not thy pen, lay all thy power. But I must be content with my wry-cut pen, and crazed pate, and write in my usual dull, stupid way. Precious gem! it honored, in my mind, human nature. Generous soldier! thy deed shall not go unrecorded. He was dressed in an old soldier's jacket, and a mariner's hat. One of his legs was off a little below the knee, the foot of the other was off at the ankle; so he walked on his knees, which were defended with leather. Full many a knock against the hard stones, did his poor stump receive as it trailed behind him; in his right hand he had a short cane, to support his steps. Thus, the poor fellow shuffled along the street. Many idle people followed him to gaze. He did not beg, but he accepted several pence given him, by various persons. I observed a marine looking steadfastly at him, and, as he looked, a tear trickled over his cheek; every line in his sun-burned face looked pity as he put his hand into his pocket and drew out an old purse; he emptied the whole contents, about two or three shillings, into his hand, and put it into that of the maimed man. The poor fellow looked gratitude, he lifted his hat, bowed his head, and thanked him. As the marine went down the street, I saw him wipe his eyes with the back of his hand, cough, and blow his nose, as though he thought a tear disgraceful in a soldier. Thou wast wrong, generous soldier! that tear, that action, did thee more honor, in my eyes, than if thou hadst slain with thine own hand, thousands of thy fellow-men, and wast therefore called a hero. That tear, of which thou seemedst ashamed, that tear, and that act, are entered in the records of Heaven! there to be rewarded. Thou, noble veteran, wast more charitable, and more praiseworthy than a rich man, if he had given fifty pounds! Thou gavest thy little *all!*

Thou didst not deliberate on the inconvenience to thyself, but thou obeyed the virtuous impulse. In the perils of war, and the temptations of peace, God be with thee, generous marine! This happened in George street, as I returned from Stonehouse fair. There my sister Elizabeth gave me a half-penny, the only one, I believe, she had. I'll not forget it."

On hearing of the death of Napoleon Bonaparte, he wrote as follows: —

"July 6. — Learned that Napoleon Bonaparte died on the 6th of May, of a cancer in his stomach. He was ill forty days. I doubt not that the public journals, newspapers, etc., have detailed all the particulars of his exit from the theatre of the world, in which he has shone as a meteor — a meteor of destructive influence; and I shall only give a few observations on his character, according to my idea of it. That he had talents, no man who has attentively considered his conduct and character, can doubt; but such talents! He was an innate tyrant; he introduced himself to notice by his eminence in adulation and cruelty. That he was a cruel man, his conduct has always shown. Witness the dreadful bridge of Lodi, the massacre of Jaffa, and the poisoning of his own sick soldiers. He was more than suspected as the murderer of the Duke d'Enghien. I consider him as a man, who, from the earliest period of public life, was resolved to let no considerations of honor, religion, humanity, or any other consideration, interfere with his advancement. Nor did they interfere. He certainly had not always thoughts of obtaining the sovereign power; but his ambition for sovereignty arose from circumstances, step by step. After the abolition of royalty and nobility, and the declaration of equality, he was resolved to admit of no superior. That he was ungrateful, may be seen by his treatment of his former patron. One or two centuries hence, and even now — if we knew not its reality — it would be considered as an improbable fiction, belonging to the ages of romance, that a man of obscure origin should thus become the ruler of nearly all Europe — thus realize the visions of Don Quixote, and reward his Sanchos with kingdoms at his pleasure — thus spread desolation, fire and sword, where naught but peace was known before; that a man, a simple man, an unsupported man, should thus make princes crouch at his foot-stool, and should have his will obeyed as a law. How many thousands of widows and orphans has he not made? A lesser villain would have been hanged for the thousandth part of his crimes; yet he has his admirers. Notwithstanding what has been said by many to the contrary, I allow him the meed of personal courage, and that he was grateful, when he could gain nothing by being the contrary. He was a hypocrite, and an infidel; for he has, at different times, been of almost all religions, Mohamedan included. He was generous by starts, condescending, when Emperor — irritable, hasty, insolent, and choleric. It will not be considered as the less extraordinary part of his story, that, in the end, he was unfortunate — obliged to abdicate his throne, and was twice banished; but, above all, that this man — this Napoleon Bonaparte — died in his bed of a cancer, while the great and good Henry, died by the hand of an assassin, and the meek Louis died on a scaffold! On the whole, it may be said of Bonaparte, that he was a glorious villian!"

The last extract, is certainly a remarkable piece of composition, for a boy of his age to produce. It is quite a keen analysis of the Emperor's character, and shows that the author's reading had not been in vain.

As we shall have occasion hereafter to quote from his Journal, the foregoing extracts must suffice for the present. We will give a specimen of his poetry, however, which, though not of high order, is nevertheless indicative of poetical taste and talent. From a piece addressed to a young lady who won his affections after he left the work-house, we extract the following: —

"In silence, I have walked full long
Adown life's narrow, thorny vale,
Deaf to the melody of song,
And all music to me mute,
From the organ's rolling peal,
To the gay burst, or mournful wail
Of harp, and psaltery, and lute.
Heaven's dread answer I have heard
In thunder to old ocean's roar,
And while the elements conferred,
Their voices shook the rock-bound shore: —
I 've listened to the murmuring streams,
Which lulled my spirit into dreams,
Bright hopes, and fair imaginings;
But false as all that fancy flings
Upon a page where pain and strife
Make up the history of life:
And so, beneath o'ershadowing trees,
I 've heard leaves rustle in the breeze,
Which brought me the melodious tale
Of the all vocal nightingale,
Or else the cushet's coo of pride,
O'er his own new-mated bride.
Yes, I have heard thee, Nature! thee,

In all thy thousand voices speak,
Which *now* are silent, all to me.
Ah, when shall this long silence break,
And all thy tides of gladness roll
In their full torrent on my soul?

"But as the snows which long have lain
On the cold tops of Lebanon,
Melt in the glances of the sun,
And, with wild rush, into the plains,
Haste down, with blessings in their train:
So, Mary, gilded by thine eye,
Griefs melt away, and fall in streams
Of hope into the land of dreams,
And life's inanities pass by
Unheeded, without tear or sigh."

CHAPTER IX.

KEY TO CHARACTER.

The last entry of his Journal in 1821—Furnishes a key to his character—A boy with twenty-five cents—How Kitto spent his tenpence at the Fair—His marked Self-Denial—Half for Paper and Books—A third for Benevolence—The Five poor little Girls—A Beautiful Picture—Case of the poor Negro in Boston—B—B—Carried a tenth home.

THE last entry of his Journal, in 1821, is worthy of particular attention. It furnishes us with a key to his character full as satisfactory as anything we find elsewhere. Yet, it is only a dry account of his expenses on the day of a public Fair. It reads as follows: —

"November 10.—It has been Fair this week. I had tenpence; I spent of it but one halfpenny, in the gratification of my palate, as follows: —

Mince-pie, - - - - - - -	0 1-2	*d.*
Paper, - - - - - - - -	3	"
Books, - - - - - - -	2	"
Gave halfpenny, each, to five little children,	2 1-2	"
Gave to B. B., - - - - - -	1	"
Left, - - - - - - -	1	"
Total,	10	*d.*

One such small transaction as this, in which a youth acts himself, furnishes a better index to his true character than many more important things. Give a boy twenty-five cents, more or less,— a faithful record of his manner of spending it, will disclose his real qualities better than his appearance in the house of worship, or in the presence of superiors. For he follows his inclinations in spending the money, and thereby exhibits the tendencies of his heart. If love of pleasure predominates over the love of books, the greater part of his funds will go for pleasure. If he delights to gratify his appetite more than to cultivate his mind, sweetmeats and cakes will receive the first attention. So with other qualities, he may possess — the way in which the money goes will be about sure to disclose them. This is especially true when the money is held for use on some holiday. Then the young expect to enjoy a liberty beyond that extended on ordinary days. If pennies are denied them at other times, they expect more or less of them on these occasions. They will use them as they please, too; for this belongs to the freedom of festive days.

Now, we have such an index to Kitto's character, in the record we have extracted from his journal.

He had tenpence at his command on the morning of a public holiday, and he could use them as he pleased. It was an occasion of great joy to the young people of Plymouth, and probably few of them had a penny left, when the day was over. Let us consider how Kitto spent his money on that gala-day.

In the first place, only a halfpenny was laid out to gratify his appetite. This was but a twentieth part of his tenpence. Although his daily fare was that of a pauper, he did not think mainly of pleasing his palate. It was a day for sweetmeats, with most of the boys; but to him, there was something sweeter than candies. A piece of mince-pie, he would take as a kind of compromise between hunger and thirst for knowledge. But paper, and books, and the luxury of doing good, occupied his thoughts. The height of his ambition was to possess the means of intellectual culture. Therefore, he spent just half of his money for paper and books, threepence for the former, and twopence for the latter. Not a very heavy outlay, to be sure, but large in proportion to the amount possessed. Few scholars are able, or disposed, to lay out half of their property in books. Yet young Kitto did this as the most satisfactory way of spending the holiday. The fact shows that self-denial was a prominent element of his character. For, it is probable that he was tempted, with the other boys, by the confectionery and countless dainties which the occasion offered. We cannot suppose that he had no longings after niceties and nicknacks, for even young paupers have a taste for these. But he was willing to forego the pleasure of possessing these, for the sake of having materials for writing, and books for reading. Very few youth are prepared to exercise such self-denial as this. A large part of them exhaust their means, on special occasions, in pandering to appetite. They present an unenviable appearance, in contrast with self-denying John Kitto.

In the second place, he gave away more than a third of his tenpence, and this was evidently the best part of the Fair to him, except the books and paper. It was better than the mince-pie, if we may judge from the amount expended for the latter. Read the record over and over.

"*Gave half-penny each to five little girls.*"

Was there ever anything more beautiful than this? A deaf youth, from the poor-house, with tenpence in his pocket, for a good time at the Fair, giving one-fourth of it to five poor, little girls! The name of the millionaire, who contributes ten or twenty thousand dollars to some benevolent object, is trumpeted from Maine to Louisiana; and yet his deed is less illustrious than that of John Kitto. For he does not give a tenth, or twentieth part of his possessions, while this generous lad gave *one-fourth* of his!

Let imagination portray, if possible, this unusual picture. See him, the poor, deaf boy, permitted to join the multitude on a festal day, sauntering along the streets at his pleasure. Tenpence is all the money he can command for the day. Other boys of his age may have ten times that amount to expend in pleasure, but he is rich, with even this little sum. Yonder come five little girls, perhaps without a farthing to spend. They are poor, and their tale of poverty is told by their miserable apparel. Rich gentlemen and ladies, in their broadcloth and satins, pass by without casting upon them a pitying glance. They know nothing, by experience, of the trials of being poor. But Kitto has a fellow-feeling with the little wanderers. His eye falls upon them, and he knows that they dwell in penury. He understands their feelings, as they walk the streets where there is enough of every thing, yet nothing for them. His heart feels for them. He would rather see them enjoying a halfpenny's worth of the good things around them, than to enjoy the same himself. So, obeying the virtuous impulse, as he said, of the generous soldier, he divided a quarter part of his *all* among these little daughters of want. Noble youth! Tender sensibilities expand thy soul, and the heart of a Howard beats within thy breast! Earth pines for want of such sympathizing spirits to lift up the fallen, and weep with those that weep. O, that more like thee, were formed to mitigate the sorrows of mankind, and bear joy and gladness to the abodes of want! How many saddened hearts would break forth into singing, and how many habitations would ring with accents of joy! Alas, for the painful thought, that hearts like thine are as angels' visits, few and far between!

It is sometimes the case, that we meet with such remarkable examples of benevolence among the poorest poor. A writer, who visited the city of Boston a few years since, relates, that as he was passing down Hanover street, one day, he saw a negro sitting upon a pile of wood, which he had just sawed, eating a few fragments of bread which had just been given to him. He devoured them with a keen relish, and seemed scarcely to realize that it was humble fare. A short distance from him, there stood a wretched white woman, watching his movements with the deepest interest. The man was curious to know the cause of her apparent interest in the negro's dinner, and he stopped to watch them. The remainder of the narrative we give in his own words:—

"The wood-sawyer, noticing her fixed look, asked her, what she wanted.

"Pointing to the meal, spread upon the log, she replied, 'I have not eaten so much as that, for two weeks.'

"'Well, sit down here, and take a bite,' said the kind-hearted negro; '*although I ain't rich, I am generous.*'

"With tears in her eyes, that seemed, just before, already sealed up from weeping, she drew near the humble table. I did not interfere, to deprive the wood-sawyer of the pleasure of completing his generous act, (for *generous* it was in him to share his only meal with another,) but after privately slipping a piece of money into the poor woman's hand, I continued my walk.

"But I could not shut out the scene from my thoughts, and the words of the African, 'not *rich* but *generous*,' kept ringing in my ears. If riches consist in the means of happiness, what a fund of wealth has a man, whom God has blessed with a sympathizing heart; for, where is there greater happiness than in blessing another? Many a man that prefaced his sumptuous dinner with a long grace, found no richer blessings at his table, that day, than did the wood-sawyer upon his log."

John Kitto, in his boyhood, belonged to that class who "ain't rich," but are "*generous*." When he was nineteen years old, he said, "I never touched a note (bank note,) in my life, nor a piece of gold coin, but once, which was ten years ago, when I was permitted to hold a seven-shilling piece in my hand for a few seconds."

One penny was given to the mysterious character, "B—— B——." Whether the recipient was man, woman, or child, a friend, or a foe, we know not. It was, doubtless, some person whom the generous giver supposed to be as needy as himself. Added to the two and a-halfpence, which he gave to the five little girls, the sum total of his gifts amounted to more than one-third of his possessions.

He carried one penny home, a tenth of all he had in the morning. This is quite unusual with boys of his age. Their pockets are generally emptied on such occasions. But Kitto resisted the temptations of the day, and carried home a penny at night. Such a boy never becomes a spendthrift. He has nobler views of life, than the spendthrift entertains. It is not an ordinary youth, who can spend a whole day among confectionery, cakes, and beautiful things, and save one of his ten pence to carry home, when the festivities are over.

CHAPTER X.

MORE SORROW.

Death of his Grandmother—Another index to his character—The Youth who joined in sports, when his mother lay dead—Extracts from Journal—Stealing softly up stairs—A view of the corpse—Outburst of grief—The Atheist—The last look—The Funeral—His feelings at the grave—The Sexton's unconcern—Visit to his Aunt—Reference to his Grandmother, and deep emotion—Shows that his is no ordinary character.

ON the 18th of April, 1821, an event transpired which overwhelmed young Kitto's heart with grief. It was the death of his beloved grandmother. We have seen that he loved her tenderly, and that he was much indebted to her, for kindly taking him under her care, when a drunken father and desolate home, gloomed his childhood. It was not surprising, then, that her death rolled a great wave of sorrow over his soul.

His journal is very interesting at this period. It reflects light upon his character, by disclosing his feelings in view of her departure. On this account, we shall quote from it at considerable length.

Let the reader bear in mind, the object for which

his attention is called to this chapter of sorrow, viz.; to furnish another key to Kitto's character. Almost any person, who will take the trouble to observe, will be impressed with the amount and correctness of the knowledge of a youth's character, acquired by noticing him in the midst of sorrow. An amiable, tender, affectionate, virtuous son, will deeply feel the loss of a near relative, particularly that of a mother. One of the opposite traits will follow the best of mothers to the grave, without exhibiting any emotion. The author well remembers a youth who joined a company of pleasure-seekers, while his dear mother lay dead at home. No person, who knew the boy, however, was surprised; for he did not sustain the character of a good son at home, or in the neighborhood. Now, a great difference will be observed among different youth in this particular, and this difference will indicate, more or less strikingly, certain characteristics. For this reason, it is well to see a youth in severe affliction, before we fully estimate his character. Such a view may modify our ideas of his worth. Kitto's journal becomes an indispensable source of information to us at this point.

"*April* 20, *Good Friday.*—Being now a little recovered from the first shock, I have, after several attempts, summoned courage to detail particulars. On Wednesday evening, when I came out (from the work-house,) I trod softly up stairs, lest I should disturb her repose; useless precaution! Aunt met me at the head of the stairs, in tears. I entered; a white sheet over the bed met my view! She was dead! Think you, I wept? I did not weep! Tears are for lesser sorrows; my sensations were too powerful for tears to relieve me. The sluices of my eyes were dried! My brain was on fire! Yet I did not weep. Call me not a monster, because I did not weep. I have not wept these four years; but I remember I *have*, when a boy, wept for childish sorrows. Then why do I not weep for this great affliction? Is not this a contradiction? Am I hard of heart? God forbid that tears should be the test, for I felt insupportable agony.

"Even to an indifferent person, the sight of a dead person awakens melancholly reflections; but when that person is connected by the nearest ties, O, then! when I saw the corpse, when I saw that those eyes, which had often watched my slumbers, and cast on me looks of affection and love, were closed in sleep eternal, those lips which had often pressed mine, which often had opened to soothe me, tell me tales, and form my infant mind, are pale, and motionless forever; when I saw that those hands that had led, carressed, and fed me, were forever stiff and motionless; when I saw all this, and felt that it was *forever*, guess my feelings, for I can not describe them! Born to be the sport of fortune, to find sorrow, where I hoped for bliss, and to be a mark for the giddy and the gay to shoot at — what I felt at the deprivation of my almost only friend, the reader can better conceive than I can describe. Yet that moment will ever be present to my recollection, to the latest period of my existence. Gone forever; that is the word of agonizing poignancy! Yet, not forever; a few short years, at most, and I *may* hope to meet her again; there is my consolation. Joyful meeting! yet a little while to bear this

"Fond, restless dream which idiots hug,
Nay, wise men flatter with the name of life,"

and we may meet again. Already I anticipate the moment, when, putting off this frail garb of mortality, and putting on the robe of immortality, of celestial brightness and splendor, in the presence of our God, we may meet again; — meet again never to part; never again to be subject to the frail laws of mortality — to be above the reach of sorrow, temptation, or sickness — to know naught but happiness — celestial happiness and heaven! Accursed be the atheist, who seeks to deprive man of his noblest privilege — of his hopes of immortality, of a motive to do good, and degrade him to a level with the beast which browses on the grass of the fields. What were man without this hope?

"I knelt and prayed for her departed spirit, to Him in whose hands are life and death, and that he would endue us with resignation to his decrees, for we know that he had a right to the life which he gave."

Kitto did not expect to attend the funeral of his grandmother, because the hour at which it was appointed, interfered with the arrangements of the work-house. He therefore took, what he thought, was the last look of the revered remains on the evening before. He thus describes it: —

"I raised the cloth; it was dusk; the features were so composed, that I was for a few moments deceived, and thought it *sleep*. I pressed my lips to her forehead; it was cold as monumental marble; cold forever! A thousand recollections rushed upon me of her tenderness, and affectionate kindness to me. She, who was now inanimate before me, was, a short time since, full of life and motion; on me her eye then beamed with tenderness, and affection dwelt in each look. When I was sick, she had watched my feverish pillow, and was my nurse; when I was a babe, she had fondled, caressed, and cherished me; in short, she had been more than a mother to me. And this friend, this mother, I was never to behold again! A thousand bitterly pleasing instances of her kindness to me, occurred to my recollection, and I found a kind of melancholly pleasure in recalling them to remembrance. I gazed on each well-known feature. I kissed her clay-cold cheek and pallid lips. I remembered how often my childish whims had vexed her. I remembered how I had sometimes disobeyed her earnest and just commands. I mentally ejaculated,

"O, that she would but come again!
I think I'd vex her so no more."

Fruitless wish! Will the grim tyrant, death, give up his prey? Will the emancipated soul return to its dreary prison? Ought I to wish it? 'No,' said reason; 'No,' said religion: such a convincing 'No,' they uttered, that I blushed for the wish."

Kitto was happily disappointed in being permitted to attend the funeral of his grandmother, and the following account of the solemn event, is found in his Journal: —

"I looked once more, and for the last time, on the corpse; once more, and for the last time, pressed her cold lips, and then she was shut from my view forever! I felt a something at my heart that moment, which baffles description. I felt as though I could have freely given my life, to prolong hers a few years. . . . . . At the appointed time, we walked in 'sad array,' behind the coffin. . . . . . There were about forty persons present. The service was read by Dr. Hawker's curate; the coffin was deposited in the grave, and covered with earth. . . . . . The moment in which the coffin, which contains the remains of a beloved relative, is hid from our sight, is perhaps, a moment of greater agony than at their demise; for then, we have still the melancholy consolation of contemplating the features of the beloved object; but when that sad and gloomy comfort is taken from us, the feelings of our loss occur with accumulated force; we consider what, a short time since, the contents of the coffin *were*, and what, in a short time, they *will* be; we consider, that in our turn, we shall be conveyed to a similar, if not to the same place, and, in our turn, be wept over with transient tears, and soon be forgotten. I thought the man almost guilty of sacrilege, and could have beaten him, who threw the earth so unconcernedly on her remains. 'Why does he not weep?' I internally asked. 'Why does not every human being join with me in lamenting her loss?' But I shall not attempt to describe my feelings; they were such, at the moment when I stood on the brink of the grave, eagerly looking on the coffin, till the earth concealed it, I shall never forget till the hand that writes this shall be as hers; and the heart that inspires it, shall cease to beat.

"When we came home, I felt a kind of faintness coming over me, and if aunt Mary had not timely rubbed my temples with cold water, I should have fainted. Grandmother is buried on the left hand side of the aisle, opposite the steeple, near the church door, (Charles Church,) beneath the head-stone erected to the memory of her grandchildren."

About six weeks after the funeral, Kitto visited his Aunt, of whom he speaks in the foregoing extracts. His reference to the visit is worthy of perusal:—

"June 10.—I have been to aunt's; was received

kindly; before I came away, uncle wrote, 'you must come out here as often as you can, for it was the dying request of your grandmother, that *we* should be kind to *you*.' And did she think of *me*, to the last; anxious for me—interested, even in death, for my welfare, and making friends for me? My only friend, my revered benefactor, my dearest grandmother, in death didst thou think of *me!* Oh, that I had been present. Yet, no; I could not have borne it. Father, receive her soul unto thy mercy, and guide my steps in the intricate path of human life, beset as it is, with thorns and briars, with temptations and sorrows, and, if it be thy pleasure that I should drink the cup of human misery and affliction to the very dregs, even then, Lord, in the midst of all, grant me strength that I may not swerve from thy will, nor murmur at thy decrees; for well I know that whatsover thou doest, is just and right, and that though thy commandments teach me to resist the dominion of my senses, they, in the end, lead to the eternal mansions of the blessed! I humbly pray thee, my God, that there I may at last arrive, through Jesus Christ, and there meet her who has gone before me."

These extracts show the intensity of Kitto's grief.

12

It is not often that we meet with such strong affection, even for the nearest relative, nor would every youth make known his angush of spirit, in this way, though it were intense. Many would seek to hide their deep emotions, as if such grief were a weakness. It is no ordinary youth, mentally or morally, who is disposed, or able, to pen such sentiments as the foregoing. These extracts alone, without additional knowledge of his character, are sufficient to convince any reader, old or young, that here is a remarkable character. Especially is this so, when it is remembered that the author is a poor deaf pauper. Intelligence, affection, constancy, grief, submission, and hope, such as are expressed in these records from his Journal, perhaps, never appeared before nor since, in the tenant of a poor-house.

CHAPTER XI.

A HARD MASTER.

Apprenticed to a Shoemaker—A cruel man—Design of Providence—Extracts from his Journal—First thoughts about leaving the Work-house—His last—The Prisoner who petitioned to return to cell—His future work-room—Discovers that his master is a tyrant—Illustrations of his cruelty—Still saved a little time from sleep for study—His volume of Essays, and this portion of his life therein—Contemplated running away—Also Suicide—Better thoughts—Measures to leave his master—His own efforts therein, and the glad surprise of the Court.

SIX months after the death of his grandmother, Kitto was apprenticed to a shoemaker, who proved himself to be a cruel wretch. He inflicted a degree of cruelty upon the boy, which, in some respects, was more insupportable than any event of his previous life. Yet Providence overruled the event, to introduce him into a sphere more congenial to his taste and feelings, where his intellectual faculties had a good opportunity to improve. For the time being, it seemed that this additional source of discouragement and suffering, would cause the unfortunate lad to infer that he was born for misery. But God often uses such agencies to introduce and accomplish his kindest purposes. So here, he made use of a "hard master" to remove a deaf pauper from the almshouse, and open the way for his introduction to literary circles.

His Journal at this time runs thus: —

"November 8. — I am no longer a work-house boy! I am an apprentice! On the 29th ult. a shoemaker came for an apprentice. After looking at our work he pitched upon me, and asked me if I would be his apprentice. I answered concisely, 'No!' Some of the boys aside, held out inducements of food, clothes, money, freedom. I pleaded deafness. He said that was no objection with him, as the last apprentice he had was deaf also. I said to the repeated question, if I would go, 'I do not care; I would as soon stay as go.' I learned that his name is Bowden, a working boot and shoemaker, residing in Higher street. He is brother-in-law to the work-house tailor. On the 30th, the tailor told me to get my father to go with me to Mr. Bowden's house, as he wanted to speak to him. I got leave to be out in the afternoon, and found father at home. I told him the news, and instructed him what to say. One thing which I told him to do, was to procure me permission from Mr. Bowden to sleep here (Nut street), as then I should have the whole night to myself. We went; Mr. Bowden was at home, and went with us to the work-house; they staid there sometime at the office. When father and I came away, he told me that objections were made to my going by Mr. Anderson, on the score that no boy but myself can perfectly make list shoes. On the 3d, Mr. B. came to the shop, and Mr. Anderson wrote on the slate, 'You must *learn* Ford before you can go;' meaning that I must *teach* Ford. They told me that I was to go apprentice on Thursday (8th.) Upon consideration of the probable advantages of being apprenticed, such as having the whole night at my disposal, the shortness of the period, but four years; the advantage of acquiring more perfection in the art there than in the work-house; food in plenty, and good clothes; all these considerations induced me to change my indifference about leaving the work-house into a desire to do so. Therefore, on Friday, (2d inst.,) I gave a paper to Mr. Barnard, expressing that desire, and soliciting his aid to my being apprenticed. *This* morning came at length. About ten o'clock, my father and Mr. Bowden came to the house. I was sent for; we went to the office; Mr. Barnard gave me the indentures to read, which were drawn out ready for signing. At eleven o'clock, we, with Mr. Barnard, went to the Guildhall, where, after waiting some time, I was called inside the bar, when the justice, Mr. R. J. Square, asked me, by signs, if I was willing to go apprentice to Mr. Bowden; when I had answered in the affirmative, he signed the indentures, and we came away. Half an hour after, we went to the work-house again; Mr. Barnard was gone to dine, therefore we waited. During this interval it occurred to me that this was the last day of my being a work-house boy; so I went to take a farewell look of the bed on which I used to sleep, the tripod on which I have sat so many hours, and the prayer-room. I shook hands, in idea, with the pump, the conduit at which I washed, the tree against which I leaned, nay, the very stones on which I walked. I felt something like regret at leaving it. Man is an accommodating animal. I had so accommodated, or accustomed myself to the work-house, that I left it with some regret. I have read of a man, who had grown old in prison; when he was liberated on the accession of a new king, he petitioned to be put in prison again. Is not this a case in point, to show that man soon accommodates himself even to misery?

"But I had not done with the work-house yet, for after waiting sometime, Mr. B. took me to his house in Higher street, and gave me a dinner of fish and potatoes; after which, we went to the work-house again, and I was sent to fetch father. We remained some time in the office, when Mr. Barnard put the seal of the house to my indentures, and Mr. Bowden made his mark, (he can't write) instead of a signature. Then Mr. Barnard asked me what clothes I had, and then gave Mr. B. an order for a hat, jacket and trousers, which was delivered to the matron. I then took a final leave of the hospital, and we went to Mr. Bowden's house again, when I was aproned and seated, and set to rip off the old top of a boot. Father then left me. Now let me describe the room in which I am to spend so much time. No, but I will not, upon second thought; only just say that it is a front room on the ground floor, situated in Higher street; the furniture is good, among which is a clock and several canary birds; they have at home one child about seven or eight years old, and they have also a journeyman. They gave me supper about eight o'clock, and I came away then."

Thus much for the beginning of Kitto's life as an apprentice. We have it in his own words, and can judge therefrom of his feelings as he entered this new sphere. He was not long in discovering, however, that he had a tyrant for a master. His journal is very explicit upon this point. We will quote from it, and thus let him tell his own story.

The first record in 1822, is a tale of wretchedness: —

"January 10.— O misery, art thou to be my only portion! Father of mercy, forgive me, if I wish I had never been born! O, that I were dead, if death were an annihilation of being, but as it is not, teach me to *endure* life; to *enjoy* it, I never can. In short, mine is a severe master, rather cruel. As I intend to (partly, if not quite) discontinue this Journal for some years, I will give a brief retrospect of what has taken place since November 8th.

"November 12.—Mr. Anderson came to the shop. They want me back again. Ford is not perfect. Mr. B. would not part with me.

. . . .

"November 29.—First blow! threw a shoe in my face! I made a wry stich.

"December 4.—Birthday. 6th.—Struck again.

"December .7—Again! I could not bear it. Had a box on the ear, a slap on the face. I did not weep in April (at his grandmother's decease,) but I did at this unkind usage. I did all in my power to suppress my inclination to weep, till I was almost suffocated. Tears of bitter anguish and futile indignation fell upon my work, and blinded my eyes. I sobbed convulsively. I was half mad with myself, for suffering him to see how much I was affected. Fool, that I was! O, that I were again in the workhouse!

"December 12.—My head ached, and yet they kept me at work till six o'clock, when they let me come away. I could eat nothing.

. . . .

"January 14.—He threw the pipe in my face, which I had accidentally broken. It hit me on the temple, and narrowly missed my eyes.

"January 16.—I held the thread too short; instead of telling me to hold it longer, he struck me on the hand with the hammer, (the iron part.) Mother can bear witness that it is much swelled; not to mention many more indignities I have received; many, many more; again, this morning, I have wept. What is the matter with my eyes? I here leave off this Journal till some other change, or extraordinary misfortune takes place."

It should be remarked that, while Kitto was subjected to this unmerciful treatment, working for his employer *sixteen*, and even *eighteen* hours a day, he continued to redeem some time from sleep, for intellectual improvement. Although returning home from his work weary, and often exhausted, he persevered in making a little progress daily, in his books. It was only a craving thirst for knowledge, accompanied with indomitable perseverance and untiring in-industry, that could enable a person to study at all, in these trying circumstances. Kitto possessed these qualities; and therefore, by self-imposed tortures he added daily to his store of knowledge.

A few years after, he published a small volume of Essays, one of which, is this trying chapter of his experience, under an assumed name. As it was published when he was only twenty years of age, it is well worthy of attentive perusal.

"At the age of seventeen, circumstances, which it is unnecessary to detail, placed William Wanley under the absolute power of an individual. This individual abused the authority he possessed; and if it was not his design to make William miserable, he at least pursued exactly the same method which he must have done, if he had had that object in view.

"Wanley was a being possessed of sensibilities and ideas rather above the situation he occupied. He was feelingly alive to insult and oppression, and often did convulsive sobs, and the tumultuous throbbings of his heart, betray his emotions, although no tear was seen on his cheek, as he smarted beneath the lash of persecution. . . . . . His condition was unsupportable. He sought some remedy, but could find none; for all his endeavors to please and give satisfaction, had no influence in ameliorating his situation. The idea of flight suggested itself, but was soon rejected, and from that of self-destruction when it occurred, he started with horror. Subsequently, however, the thought of suicide frequently recurred, and by becoming familiar, lost all its terrors; and ultimately he resolved on the act, and fixed the night on which it should be executed. Nothing occurred in the interval but what tended to confirm his resolution, and he spent the former part of the appointed night in writing a letter to a friend, from which the following are a few detached extracts: —

"At my first outset into life, I deemed the world a scene of universal philanthropy, and I felt confident of meeting the smile of protection and encouragement from my superiors, and the embraces of fraternal kindness from my equals. I had heard tales of sorrow, and read of beings who had fallen the victims of wounded feelings, but I could not comprehend it; and I made the internal inquiry, 'What is sorrow? What is grief?'

"Then I was a child, and knew not of the world and its ways. To me *then*, the whole universe seemed dressed in smiles, and all was happiness and joy. The sun shed his benignant rays alike on all, exhilerating universal nature with his presence, and the fields were gay with verdure and with flowers. All *then* was lovely, all was beautiful. And is it not still so? Yes; but not to me. Every thing I view partakes of the somber tone of my feelings, and, though the sun continues to shine, I am not of the number who delight in his beams.

"There was a time when I was gay, and tasted harmless pleasure. But now, I ask, 'What is joy? What is happiness?' for I remember it no more. O, ye days of careless boyhood, why did ye flee so swiftly? Why must the tender plant, before it acquires strength to stem the storms of adversity, be crushed by the foot of the oppressor?

. . . . . . "I intended to have made a formal complaint to you; but as I know it to be impossible that you should fully enter into my feelings and situation, I feared that you think mine *ideal* miseries, because you could not appreciate them. I apprehended, also, that continual claims on your friendship, would tire out, particularly as you have taken no active steps, in consequence of the information which, at various times, I have communicated to you. And when I contemplated the formidable appendage of seals and signătures affixed to the instruments, by which I am enslaved, I doubted whether it was ever in your power to redress my grievances. . . . . .

"And what became of Wanley? will be the natural inquiry after perusing these extracts. Did he succeed in the object which he undoubtedly attempted? I am glad that this little narrative must be deficient in the interest which it would derive from so tragical a conclusion.

"He still lives, and contemplates with horror his former attempts, and the fallacious sophistry with who he endeavored to silence the voice of conscience. He lives to thank that merciful Providence which preserved him from the actual commission of such a deed of guilt; though he fears that time will never eradicate from his mind that tone of thought which was acquired in the days of his misery and distress."

It appears from this narrative, that Kitto so keenly felt the wrongs inflicted upon him by his cruel master, as to determine first, upon flight, and second, upon *suicide.* It was well that Satan did not gain such complete dominion over him as to lead him to perpetrate the latter guilty deed. But we speak of the fact, because it indicates the intensity of his mental suffering under the ill-usage of a heartless man. Great must be the misery of a sane person, who resolves upon self destruction, to escape from earthly wrongs and distress.

But did Kitto enter no complaint against his employer to his father, or other friend? the reader inquires. We reply, that he endured much before he complained to any one, of his unkind treatment. He feared that his complaints would not be appreciated. But finally, he resolved to make known his grievances, both at home, and to his friends at the work-house. This led to the rupture of his apprenticeship, and his return to the work-house, within six months from the time he was indentured to Bowden. The part which Kitto acted in bringing about this result, introduced him to public notice, as a youth of uncommon abilities, and secured for him many literary benefactors, through whose patronage he was thereafter enabled to glean knowledge in the fields of science and literature. We spoke in the beginning of this chapter, of the hand of God in this result. It occurred on this wise.

Through the agency of Mr. Barnard, his case was brought before the magistrates, and his employer was summoned to appear and show cause, if possible, why his apprentice should not be immediately removed. As Kitto was deaf, and not much inclined to oral communication, he was required to make his complaints in writing. He did this so readily, and with such correct diction, that the whole Bench were surprised. It not only secured for him a favorable verdict, but also enlisted the interest of the Court in his future advancement. It was this circumstance which had not a little to do with his promotion afterwards. Thus his brief connection with the unfeeling Bowden was overruled by Divine Providence for his best good.

CHAPTER XII.

HIS SECOND STUDY.

Scene in a Bookseller's Shop—Mr. Harvey's curiosity excited—Public interest awakened in Kitto—Subscription in his behalf—His Essays in the Plymouth Weekly Journal—The Circular to the public—Removal from the Poor House—Admitted to the Public Library—His "Second Study," and description of it—A dear Retreat.

ONE day, a distinguished mathematician, by the name of Harvey, went into a bookseller's shop on business. While he was there, a youth entered, and immediately opened a communication with the proprietor, by writing on a piece of paper. Mr. Harvey was somewhat impressed by the appearance of the lad, and inquired of the bookseller, after the youth went out, what was the meaning of the scene just witnessed. The bookseller told him that the visitor was a poor, work-house boy, who had a great thirst for knowledge, and that he came to borrow a book which had been promised him.

Mr. Harvey was so much interested by the fact that a young pauper should frequent a bookstore, to gratify his thirst for knowledge, that he determined to know something more of the boy. He made inquiries of different persons concerning him, and soon became satisfied that Kitto was a remarkable youth. He adopted measures at once to bring his case to the notice of literary gentlemen. Nor did he experience any difficulty in this; for the manliness and talents which he had exhibited in the court room, as stated in the last chapter, had won many friends, who were ready to co-operate in placing Kitto where he might enjoy good advantages for mental improvement.

A subscription was opened in behalf of the pauper student, and many very generously contributed. In addition to money, books, paper and pens, were given by those interested in his intellectual culture.

At the same time, one of the proprietors of the Plymouth Weekly Journal, who had seen some of Kitto's composition, offered to insert an Essay from his pen in his popular sheet. Accordingly, an article on Happiness, soon made its appearance. This was followed immediately by two others on Home and Contemplation. These articles were read by the public with eager interest, and nothing else scarcely, was talked about in the town but the wonderful pauper. Every body wanted to see him, while hundreds desired to assist him. He was at once brought into notice, and all persons agreed that it would be quite too bad to suffer such abilities to be confined in a poor-house.

Several gentlemen of distinction associated themselves to be his future guardians. At the commencement of their efforts in his behalf, they published the following circular, which is an important document at this point: —

"The attention of the public has lately been drawn, by some Essays published in the Plymouth Weekly Journal, to the very extraordinary talents of John Kitto, who is now a pauper in the Plymouth work-house. He is about eighteen years of age, and has been nearly four years in the work-house, to which he was reduced by the inability of his parents to maintain him, after his having lost his hearing by a fall from a house in Batter street, where he was employed as an attendant on the masons. The loss of hearing has been accompanied with other bodily infirmities; but he has been thus so entirely thrown on the resources of his own mind, that he has cultivated his intellectual faculties with singular success, and gives promise of making very considerable attainments. An inquiry into his conduct, and general character, has proved most satisfactory to the undersigned, who are thus led to believe that he must greatly interest those who feel for the difficulties under which virtue and talents labor when they have to struggle with poverty and misfortune. He has of late been employed as a shoemaker, in the work-house, and in that capacity he has given proofs of great skill and industry; but it seems desirable that he should be placed in a situation more consistent with his feelings and abilities, and to which his deafness might not render him incompetent. It has been suggested that, as a temporary measure, application should be made to the Committee of the Plymouth Public Library, to employ him as a sub-librarian; and that a sum might be raised, by small subscriptions, to enable him to obtain board and lodging in some decent family, until something permanently advantageous should be suggested. In the mean time, although he could not be in the receipt of a salary, he would have opportunities of improving himself, and would be enabled to direct the powers of his mind to those pursuits in which he is so well qualified to excel, and, in which, perhaps, the world may find his usefulness, and he himself a merciful and abundant compensation for all his deprivations. Great reliance may be placed on his industrious habits, and it is confidently believed that small contributions from several individuals, would enable him to get over the chief impediments to success, in a way for which he seems so peculiarly well-qualified. The undersigned, who have carefully examined into his character and acquirements, are anxious to give the strongest testimony in his behalf, and will receive with great pleasure any contributions, pledging themselves to use the utmost discretion in their power, in the application of any money which may be intrusted thus to their management.

"JOHN HAWKER,
HENRY WOOLLCOMBE,
WILLIAM EASTLAKE,
THOMAS STEWART,
JOHN TINGCOMBE,
GEORGE HARVEY,
ROBERT LAMPEN.

Plymouth, 26*th June*, 1823."

After some deliberation, it was decided to remove Kitto from the work-house, and place him where he could have ample time for reading and study, having access to the Public Library. On July 17, 1823, he left the poor-house, and went to board and lodge with

Mr. Barnard. His removal was recorded as follows by the Guardians of the Poor: —

"John Kitto discharged, 1823, July 17. Taken out under the patronage of the *literati* of the town."

He spent several hours each day at the Public Library, which he was wont to call his "Second Study." He gives the following description of the room he occupied there.

"It was a large and lofty room, lighted by a lantern in the roof. It had no funiture beyond a large table and a great number of arm-chairs. It was properly the committee room of a public library, but, as the committee made use of it but once in the month, for a few hours, and as I used it alone at all other times, I am authorized to call it my study. The folding-doors of this room opened into a good library of some twelve thousand well-selected volumes, among which I might freely revel at large, from morning to night. But I did not revel. I do not know what whim led me to confine my attention almost excluively to metaphysics. The novels there, the poems, and the periodicals, slept quietly on their shelves for me. I do not care a pin now for metaphysics; yet, upon the whole, I do not now regret the attention I gave to this study, as I believe it has been useful in its ultimate effects. It made me doubt; and, in human studies, a state of doubt is probably a good one for a student. Different as the certain facts of geometry and the uncertain and dark guesses of metaphysics are, the latter are perhaps, the best exercises of the mind for those who have no taste for the former, which I confess, I never had. I could never cross the Asses' bridge without falling into the water. That head-breaking subject, the origin of our ideas, chiefly interested me, and the uncertainty in which I was, after all my labor, left, as to whether we had any innate ideas, or any ideas at all, gave me a disgust of metaphysical inquiry, so that I have, I believe, not looked into any metaphysical work since. I never retained a taste for any study after finding that no certain results could be obtained. Yet in this line of inquiry, like the alchemists in their search for the philosopher's stone, and the elixir of life, I obtained some useful knowledge, acquired some useful habits, and drew some useful conclusions; but whether these were worthy the labor expended, is another question.

"Perhaps my mind dwells on this study with less of detailed interest than on any other; and this, perhaps, because I had no strict propriety in it, and could not arrange things there as I pleased. It was not my own. The mind, therefore, recurs rather to the golden opportunities of study enjoyed there, than to any local attachment connected with the study itself. Thus, in one point of view, it is more interesting to me than any other place, for I have never had such opportunities since, and, in other points, less so than any other."

Thus much for Kitto's "Second Study." It differed very much from his first study in the attic of his father's humble abode. It is doubtful, however, if it had much more to do with his early habits, and his distinguished success. Yet it was a very dear retreat to him. He spent many happy hours among the numerous volumes of that public library. It was a great change for him, even more than he had reason to expect. He regarded the privilege in this light, and improved every moment with untiring industry.

CHAPTER XIII.

A COMPARISON.

Which is the greater obstacle to success, deafness, or blindness? —Two facts to be noticed—(1.) The Blind are generally happy—Testimony of Rev. W. H. Milburn, the Blind Lecturer—Happier than the Deaf, because have reason to be—Lines by a Blind old Lady, of Philadelphia—Testimony of Dr. Woodbridge, the Blind Preacher—(2.) Many Blind people distinguish themselves in different callings—Deaf do not—Homer and Milton—Saunderson and Euler—Blind more successful than Deaf, because fewer obstacles in their way—Testimony of Dr. Guilleé, Superindendent of Blind Asylum, at Paris—Of Dr. Watson, Manager of a Deaf and Dumb Asylum—Testimony of Holman, the Blind Traveller—Dr. Reid's Remark.

PERHAPS the reader has been saying to himself, "Well, Kitto had a good pair of eyes left, so that his condition was far preferable to that of the blind." It is generally supposed that the loss of sight is a far greater calamity, and subjects the sufferer to far greater obstacles to success, than the loss of hearing. It is worth while, then, to stop and consider the question: Which is the greater calamity, deafness or blindness? It is only by properly settling this point that we can appreciate Kitto's success.

In the first place, there are two facts to be noticed. One is, that blind persons are usually happy. This cannot be said of the deaf. Rev. W. H. Milburn, the distinguished blind lecturer, says: "Yet have I never seen or read of a morbid or unhappy blind man. A tranquil hope, an assurance imparting quiet animation, renders tolerable this great calamity. Amid the trials of their lot, the ample resources of our nature, latent and undreamed of in ordinary life, vindicate the blessed compensations which attest the government of love."

Again: the same writer, speaking of the things suited to cheer the blind, says, "Cheerfully do I turn me now to look upon some of the compensations which underlie and bless the lot of those who sit in darkness. Forlorn, indeed, and wretched, does the state at first sight seem. Shut out from vision of mountains and oceans; without a message from sun or stars; cheered by no pleasant sight of corn-fields, or meadows dotted with flocks and herds; unused to the dreamy twilight of the deep forest, or the silvery gleam of the brook, as it breaks into sunshine; in any alphabet by which to interpret the craft of the builder, or the miracles of painting, or sculpture, the condition of the blind seems dismal enough —

quite enough to justify the pathetic recital of blind Milton: —

> 'Thus with the year
> Seasons return; but not to me returns
> Day, or the sweet approach of even or morn,
> Or sight of vernal bloom, or summer's rose,
> Or flocks or herds, or human face divine.
> But cloud instead, and everduring dark
> Surrounds me. From the cheerful ways of men
> Cut off; and, for the book of knowledge fair,
> Presented with a universal blank
> Of Nature's works, to me expunged and rased,
> And wisdom, at one entrance, quite shut out.'

"I have already had occasion to hint at the exquisite training imparted to the other senses, by reason of the absence of this princely one; the delicacy of the touch, amounting almost to the development of another sense, so quick do the nerves become in their apprehension of forms and distances. But the *balance of faculties is maintained chiefly through the ear; and, upon reflection, is it not through this organ, that the largest contributions to happiness are made from without?*"

In this extract, we have a graphic description of the privations of the blind; but the closing lines direct the reader's attention to a greater blessing that is left, as a good reason for that cheerful, happy frame of mind, which usually characterizes this class.

Mr. Milburn here asserts, that "the largest contributions to happiness" are made through the *ear*. If this be true, the blind have more reason to be happy than the deaf.

The following beautiful lines are expressive of the content and peace of a blind old lady of Philadelphia, whose name is Elizabeth Lloyd. They have often been ascribed to Milton; but it is now known that this excellent woman is the author: —

"I am old and blind —
Men point to me as smitten by God's frown —
Afflicted and deserted of my kind;
Yet I am not cast down.

"I am weak, yet strong;
I murmur not that I no longer see;
Poor, old, and helpless, I the more belong,
Father, supreme, to thee.

"Oh, merciful One!
When men are furthest, then thou art most near;
When friends pass by, my weakness shun,
Thy chariot I hear.

"Thy glorious face
Is leaning towards me; and its holy light
Shines in upon my lonely dwelling-place,
And there is no more night.

"On my bended knee
  I recognize thy purpose clearly shown;
My vision thou hast dimmed, that I MAY see
  Thyself, thyself alone.

"I have naught to fear —
  This darkness is the shadow of thy wing,
Beneath it I am almost sacred; here
  Can come no evil thing.

"O, I seem to stand,
  Trembling, where foot of mortal ne'er hath been,
Wrapt in the radiance of that sinless land
  Which eye hath never seen!

"Visions come and go —
  Shapes of resplendent beauty round me throng;
From angel lips I seem to hear the flow
  Of soft and holy song.

"It is nothing now;
  When heaven is opening on my sightless eyes;
When airs from Paradise refresh my brow;
  That earth in darkness lies.

"In a purer clime
  My being fills with rapture; waves of thought
Roll in upon my spirit — strains sublime,
  Break over me unsought.

"Give me now my lyre:
  I feel the stirrings of a gift divine;
Within my bosom glows unearthly fire;
  Lit by no skill of mine."

The following opinion of Dr. Woodbridge, the distinguished blind preacher, is in point, both as relating to the happy spirit of the blind, and the view that deafness is a greater calamity than blindness: —

"I have sometimes heard ministers, when I have been in the pulpit with them, pray that God would cheer me in my great and long solitude. This superficial view of my situation has amused and surprised me. I have been one of the most social of human beings, and have been, in a much greater degree than common, mixed up and identified with my fellow-beings. This has been well-known by all who have been familiar with me. . . . . .

An erroneous method of conceiving of the external senses is very common. The philosophical idea of the different senses is, that they are so many windows through which the soul looks out; and if any window is darkened, the soul learns to seek its information through other windows. It is a direct and easy way to mark the expression of another person, by looking at his countenance and manner; and, because it is easier to use the eye in discovering the expression of another, the ear is not much relied on. *But the ear, after all, is a more acute and faithful sen-*

tinel than the eye. The feelings of the inner man ray themselves out through the voice more perfectly than through the varying expressions of the eye. *I can interpret a man's mind more accutely through his voice than I could through his face, if I had the eyes of an Argus. I have often surprised people by speaking of the expression of their eyes, which I perceived from the tones of their voice.* . . . .

"In regard to the loss of my sight, it is undoubtedly considered by observers, a great calamity; but God has thrown in counterbalancing advantages, so that I do not, and never have, regretted the event. It has been the occasion of much good in this life, and, I trust, will send forward a beneficial influence over my journey in the life to come. In the dark inn of my mortality, I look out of the window, and the path before me seems covered with summer light."

Again: "I have been through life uniformly cheerful. Indeed, my life has, perhaps, been as bright with happiness as the life of any other man.

. . . .

"I have always made my calm, domestic scenes bright and gladsome; and I do not believe the sun has shone upon a happier house than my own."

The blind then, as a class, are happy. The fact indicates that they have sources of enjoyment left to them, after the organ of vision has been destroyed. It shows that they are not subjected to the severest affliction, otherwise they could not be so cheerful.

The other things of which we spoke as bearing upon the question whether the blind are more afflicted than the deaf, is, that many blind people have distinguished themselves in different pursuits, while this has been true of only a few of the deaf. There is scarcely any pursuit in which some blind persons have not become adepts. In all the arts and sciences they have made wonderful achievements, almost every person will recall some one of this class, who has made considerable improvement in some calling; but he does not know of one, probably, among the deaf, of whom this could be said. Two of the greatest poets who ever lived, were blind; they were Homer and Milton. Few philosophers were ever more famed than Saunderson and Euler, both of whom were blind, the former from childhood, and the latter from early manhood. Even in mechanics, several of this class have made remarkable progress, so that we find blind architects constructing bridges, drawing plans of roads, and overseeing the projected work to the satisfaction of commissoners. It is not necessary to particularize here. In a subsequent chapter we shall give some examples of distinguished success among the blind. It is sufficient for our present purpose to state the fact that this class have triumphed over obstacles which the deaf have seldom, if ever, surmounted. This indicates that deafness is a greater obstacle to success than blindness.

Here, then, are the two facts to be considered: — (1) the blind are happier than the deaf; (2) they often triumph over obstacles which the deaf cannot surmount. These two facts alone, without any additional testimony, are sufficient to lead the reflecting mind to conclude that the deaf labor under the greater privations. Add to this the testimony of certain physicians, and of the blind themselves, and there is little doubt that the loss of hearing was a worse privation to Kitto, than the loss of his eyes would have been.

Dr. Guilleé, who had charge at the time, of the Institution for the Blind at Paris, says, "Which are the most unhappy, the deaf-mutes or the blind? People ask us this every day. We shall resolve it to the advantage of the blind, because we think them, in fact, less unhappy. Strangers to all that passes around them, the deaf-mutes, who see every thing, enjoy nothing. Like Tantalus, whom the fable represents to us as devoured by inextinguishable thirst in the midst of water, they are continually subjected to cruel privations. An insurmountable barrier separates them from the rest of men; they are alone in the midst of us, unless we know that artificial language which the talent and charity of their ingenious teachers have created for them. The custom which they have of reading the physiognomy, is very often a subject of ever additional anxiety to them; they do not always divine aright; doubt and uncertainty increase their anxiety and suspicions; a serious cast, which resembles sadness, then invades their countenance, and proves that with us they are in their state of real privation. Obliged to concentrate themselves within themselves, the activity of their imagination is thus greatly augmented; and, as attention and judgment follow necessarily the perception of ideas, they exhaust themselves immensely. Therefore, one sees few deaf-mutes in the lists of longevity, because the frictions are too lively, and, to use an expression common, but exact, 'the sword wears away the scabbard.'

"More favored than these melancholly children of silence, the blind enjoy all the means of conversation with other men; no obstacle hinders them from hearing or being heard, since the ear, which has been so philosophically defined as the vestibule of the soul, is always open for them. The exchange is rapidly made, because they speak the vulgar language. It would be easy to prove that the blind have shared other advantages over the deaf-mutes."

Dr. Watson, the manager of a Deaf and Dumb Asylum, says, "Take a boy of nine or ten years of age, who has never seen the light, and you will find him conversable, and ready to give long narratives of past occurrences, &c. Place by his side a boy of the same age, who has had the misfortune to be born deaf, and observe the contrast. The latter is insensible to all you say; he smiles, perhaps, and his countenance is brightened by the beams of holy light; he enjoys the face of nature, nay, reads with attention your features, and, by sympathy, reflects your smile or frown. But he remains mute; he gives no account of past experience, or of future hope. You attempt to draw something of this sort from him; he tries to understand, and to make himself understood; but he cannot; he becomes embarrassed; you feel for him, and turn away from a scene too trying, under the impression, that of these two children of misfortune, the comparison is greatly in favor of the blind, who appears by his language to enter into all your feelings and conceptions, while the unfortunate deaf-mute can hardly be regarded as a rational being."

Here we have the concurring testimony of the conductor of a Blind Asylm, and the Principal of a Deaf and Dumb Institution, upon this subject. They agree that deafness creates more obstacles in the path of success than blindness.

Mr. Holman, the well known blind traveller, says that he once entertained the opinion, in common with others, that blindness was more to be dreaded than deafness; but that after he was visited by the terrible calamity, his views upon the subject were entirely changed. He declared that, if a choice of the two evils were left to himself, he should unhesitatingly choose blindness. He goes on to give his reasons as follows: —

"I can still enjoy society, and take a part in every ordinary occupation of life with as much facility and pleasure as previous to my calamity, with the exception of reading, or going about by myself in a strange place. It may be supposed that I sustain a great disadvantage in not being able to observe the countenances of those with whom I converse, but this is by no means so important to me as persons are apt to imagine; for the tone of voice, the manner, and my own imagination, combine to compensate the deficiency; however, the greatest recompense that we receive for our misfortune is the universal sympathy of mankind, who believe that blindness outweighs all other afflictions; all blind persons are aware of this, and I am persuaded that it forms the basis of that kindliness and constant cheerfulness in society, for which the blind are so peculiarly remarkable. With the deaf, the case is reversed, not from the intentional neglect of the world, but because it is difficult to entertain deaf persons without wholly concentrating general attention, a consideration which is of itself sufficient to deter most persons from the attempt; but were this not enough, the necessity of raising the voice to an extraordinary pitch, proves to many, physically distressing; and in those extreme cases where recourse must be had to a peculiar method of conversation, few possess a knowledge of the art so accurate as to use it with requisite rapidity. Hence, the deaf, being involuntarily shunned, learn to look upon society with invidious eyes; the mirthful they regard as satirists, the grave as detractors, and all the world as if it were estranged from them. A little reflection might convince them that no single person can engross the attention of a crowd, nor even of a circle, beyond a passing moment; but it is almost useless to address feelings so strongly biased by circumstances; and with suspicion, the offspring of neglect, it would be folly to argue."

It appears from the foregoing, that the following passage from Dr. Reid's "Inquiry into the Human Mind" must be true: "*Sight discovers almost nothing which the blind may not comprehend.*" By no means can this be said of the deaf.

In the next chapter, we shall cite some incidents in the life of Kitto, which illustrate the evils of deafness.

CHAPTER XIV.

INCIDENTS.

Illustrative of obstacles to success — Obstacles to entering the ordinary callings—Going up St. Paul's, and its perils—The shower of Potter's vessels in the East, and his miraculous escape—Difficulty of the Deaf conversing in company—The poor Deaf Boy's Remark—A greater privation still—He never heard the voices of his children.

THE life of every deaf person must be replete with incidents illustrative of the great privations to which he is subjected. They may not be recorded, but they nevertheless exist, to the discomfort and misery of the afflicted. There are two or three incidents of this character in the life of Kitto, to which we shall call the readers attention. Before citing these, however, it may be well to let him speak of the difficulties which hedged up his way in regard to entering upon any of the avocations of life.

He says, in his "Lost Senses," "If the reader spares one moment to take a glance over the occupations by which men live and thrive, he will be surprised to find how few there are for which the condition to which I was reduced would not operate as a serious disqualification. To all trades consisting of buying and selling, hearing is most essential; to all professions it is still more necessary; and there are not many kinds of handicraft in which it could be easily dispensed with. Still, there are some kinds in which even one who is deaf might contrive to get on, through the occasional help and ever ready sympathy, which I am happy to believe that handicraft workmen are apt to show, at any expense of time or labor, towards an afflicted brother. But even handicraft labor seemed closed against one who was deaf. The branches are few to which deafness would not be an insurmountable barrier, and in these few a premium would be necessary. And, even with a premium, who would readily encumber himself with a deaf apprentice, when he might have a choice of those in full possession of all their senses? Taking all these matters into account, it seems that the utmost usefulness to which one in this position could feasibly aspire, would be that of redeeming himself from entire uselessness by doing *something* towards his own maintenance; and that this alone would be so difficult, as, under all the circumstances, to become a great and meritorious achievement. The more carefully this matter is considered, the more providential it will appear that my attention should have been turned, so decidedly as it was, to the only means which seem really available for any large usefulness to myself and others."

Thus, at the very outset, Kitto encountered almost insurmountable obstacles. It seemed scarcely possible for him to obtain a livelihood in any trade or profession. The world had little or nothing for a deaf youth to do.

Kitto gives the following account of an adventure, later in life; and it shows some of the difficulties which the deaf meet with, even in going about: —

"I once went up St. Paul's so high as the gallery, at the top of the dome. As I was then accompanied by a friend, the adventure was accomplished without much inconvenience; and I was so much interested in the view over the great city, from the high point which had been reached, that I ventured to promise myself many more such excursions, from which air, exercise, and eye pleasure, might at once be realized. One attempt of this kind by myself was quite sufficient for me. Those who have ascended to that mysterious height, know that it is accomplished in utter darkness up sundry flights of wooden steps or stairs, with numerous turnings, and protected at the sides only by a hand-rail. Over what depths these stairs are laid, I know not; but the impression to one who could not hear, and where the darkness prevented from seeing, was, that they hung in air over some fathomless vacuum, so that if one took a false step, or slipped over the stairs, down he would go; down, down, down to the very crypts of the cathedral. . . . . . As I went up and descended this apt symbol of "ambition's ladder," many persons passed me from above and from below, of whose approach I had no intimation by voice or footstep. These were my real or imagined dangers; for while on the one hand it was only by feeling along the hand-rail that I could direct my own course, during the devious turnings of the stairs, on the other, I was in the utmost trepidation lest in my ascent I should be trodden down and hurled over by parties hurrying down from above, and of whose approach I could not know till they were close upon me; or lest that in my own descent, I should myself deal out the same doom upon those who were toiling their upward course. The latter danger was perhaps greater than the former; for those who were coming down might know by the sound of my footsteps, that some one was before them; but of the proximity of those who were meeting me in my own descent, I could have no intimation. In fact, I actually came breast to breast with several persons, who would certainly have been toppled over by the concussion, if I had descended with any of the impetus with which many others came down. . . . . . This to me seemed a greater danger — at least it affected me more strongly than any, and they are not few — that I ever incurred in all my adventures by flood or field; and when I landed safely at the bottom, I vowed never again to attempt so great a danger for so inadequate a recompense. My old experience in falling may have had some effect in producing this trepidation; for that experience was certainly not calculated to recommend this kind of operation to me, although if there seemed any chance that my hearing might be knocked in again, by such another concussion as that which knocked it out, it might appear worth my while to try it once more."

At another time, when Kitto was in foreign parts, he came nigh losing his life in consequence of his deafness. His description of the scene, in which his life became involved, is replete with interest. He was staying for a while about six miles from Constantinople, at a village on the Bosphorus. He frequently went down to Constantinople in the morning, and returned by water in the afternoon. On the day in question, he was detained by rain, so that he did not get back to the village where he was stopping until nearly dark. From this point we will let him tell his own story.

"After I had paid the fare, and was walking up the beach, the boatmen followed and endeavored to impress something upon me, with much emphasis of manner, but without disrespect. My impression was that they wanted to exact more than their fare; and, as I knew that I had given the right sum, I, with John Bullish hatred at imposition, buckled up my mind against giving one fare more. Presently the contest between us brought over some Nizan soldiers from the guard-house, who took the same side with the boatmen; for, when I attempted to make my way on, they refused to allow me to proceed. Here I was in a regular dilemma, and was beginning to suspect that there was something more than the fare in question, when a Turk, of apparently high authority, came up; and, after a few words had been exchanged between him and the soldiers, I was suffered to proceed.

"As I went on up the principal street of the village, I was greatly startled to perceive a heavy earthen vessel, which had fallen with great force from above, dashed in pieces on the pavement at my feet. Presently, such vessels descended, thick as hail, as I passed along, and were broken to shreds on every side of me. It is a marvel how I escaped having my brains dashed out; but I got off with only a smart blow between the shoulders. A rain of cats and dogs is a thing of which we have some knowledge; but a rain of potter's vessels was very much beyond the limits of European experience. On reaching the hospitable roof which was then my shelter, I learned that this was the night which the Armenians, by whom the place was chiefly inhabited, devoted to the expurgation of their houses from evil spirits, which act they accompanied, or testified, by throwing earthern vessels out of their windows, with certain cries, which served as warnings to the passengers; but the streets were, notwithstanding, still so dangerous, that scarcely any one ventured out while the operation was in progress. From not hearing these cries, my danger was of course two fold, and my escape seemed something more than remarkable; and I must confess that I was of the same opinion, when the next morning disclosed the vast quantity of broken pottery with which the streets were strewed."

He adds, "the adventures of this day will serve for a specimen of the numberless incidents, showing the sort of difficulties which a deaf man has to contend with in distant travel."

Kitto describes some of the mortifying positions he has been forced into while in company with others. The difficulty of holding conversation in the social circle, he speaks of in the following language: —

When he desires to speak, "the eyes are thrown round the circle again and again, to catch a moment when nobody else is speaking. But nothing is harder to catch than this. After long watching for the happy moment in which a sentence may be thrust in, it may seem at last to be secured. Every tongue is at rest. Then I begin, when a start of divided attention, a look, wandering from me to another, apprizes me that the ball of conversation had again been struck up in another part of the circle, in the brief interval of an eye-blink, and I find myself involved in the incivility and rudeness of having interrupted another, perhaps a lady, and have to drop, with a confusion of face, the word I had taken up, or else to give it utterance under circumstances of apology and pressure, which magnifies into mortifying importance, and therefore, renders abortive what was designed only as airy remark or jocular illustration.

"If, however, it so happens that I do succeed in launching my observation without such utter wreck at the outset, I have often the humiliation of finding that it has become stale by keeping, and that it applies to a subject which the rapid current of oral talk has left a mile behind."

It is no small privation thus to be debarred the privilege of oral communication. No person can fully appreciate this evil, without the terrible experience. The amount of happiness derived from conversation cannot be estimated; and this is denied the deaf man. A report of the Dublin Asylum contains the account of a deaf and dumb boy, who was present where some gentlemen were conversing upon a subject that deeply interested them. He watched their countenances with the utmost attention, in order to discover, if possible, what their conversation was about, but it was vain. At length he asked, by signs, to be informed of what they were conversing. The gentlemen kindly attempted to enlighten him; but the subject was so far beyond his attainments at that time, that his curiosity could not be satisfied. Finding all his efforts to understand them fruitless, the poor boy turned away with a despairing look; and, almost bursring into tears, he made use of the only few words he had learned to use and understand, "*Deaf and dumb is bad, is bad, is bad!*" Such are probably the feelings of every deaf person in the social circle.

There is another privation, of which Kitto speaks, that ought not to pass unnoticed. His own words describe it thus: — "*I never heard the voices of any of my children.* The reader, of course, knows this; but the fact, as stated in plain words, is almost shocking. Is there any thing on earth so engaging to a parent, as to catch the first lispings of his infant's tongue; or so interesting as to listen to its dear prattle, and trace its gradual mastery of speech? If there be any one thing arising out of my condition, which, more than another, fills my heart with grief, it is THIS; it is to *see* their blessed lips in motion, and to *hear* them not; and to witness others moved to smiles and kisses by the sweet peculiarities of infantile speech which are incommunicable to me, and which pass by me like the idle wind."

What a fountain of earthly bliss is here sealed up to the deaf, never more to hear the voice of a child! Let the young reader imagine, if possible, that he is never more to hear the voice of father or mother, brother or sister, and say, is it possible to estimate the greatness of this privation? How much happiness is actually added to our earthly share by this one thing — the voice of a friend. That voice is a part of himself. Its tones are peculiar to him. They belong to no one else. We know him by the sound thereof. If absent, the sound of his voice is remembered, whenever we recollect him. It is a prolific source of enjoyment to us at all times.

The privations of the deaf cited, are not of the gravest character. Kitto experienced some, more particularly connected with his efforts after knowledge, of a much more serious nature. But those presented in this chapter belong to the daily life of the deaf man. He is liable to meet them in every community, at any hour. On this account they are worthy of being pondered. In the next chapter, I propose to give some account of a deaf person, whose experience will exhibit, in a still more striking manner, the obstacles of deafness to intellectual progress.

CHAPTER XV.

YOUNG MASSIEU.

Case of young Massieu—A Pupil of Abbé Sicard—Had no idea of God until thirteen years old—Thought the heavens descended to make plants grow—Prayed to a Star for his Mother's recovery, and stoned it because she grew worse—Not know who made horse, or ox, or himself—Evidence of his superior abilities—His case like others—The Pupil in American Deaf and Dumb Asylum, who thought somebody stole his hearing—Another Pupil in Edinburgh, who thought the moon and stars were fires kindled by distant people—The American Lady who was Deaf—The little Deaf Pupil of Charlotte Elizabeth—The Deaf Frenchman who suddenly recovered his hearing at twenty-four years of age—These prove that deafness is a greater obstacle than blindness—Wherein Kitto's case differed from the foregoing.

THE celebrated Abbé Sicard had a deaf and dumb student, who received no instruction at all until he was thirteen years of age. During these thirteen years he acquired very little knowledge, showing that deafness was certainly, in his case, a greater obstacle to mental improvement than blindness usually is; for boys who can hear, acquire considerable information about men and things, by the time they are as old, although they may not attend school one day. It is impossible to find the case of a blind boy on record, who was so ignorant at thirteen. And yet young Massieu possessed remarkable mental abilities, as his subsequent career proved. His mind was active, and all his intellectual faculties were of high order. We can easily judge of the amount of knowledge he possessed, by looking at a few facts which he gives, relating to that early period of his life. Of course, after he had been under the tuition of Sicard for a season, and had acquired correct ideas of things to a certain extent, he was able to look back and see what a blank his mind was before he knew his distinguished teacher.

He had no proper idea of God. He said, "In my childhood, my father made me make prayers in gestures, evening and morning. I threw myself on my knees, I joined my hands, and *moved my lips*, in imitation of those who speak when they are praying to God. At present I know there is a God, who is the creator of heaven and earth. *In my childhood I adored the heavens, not God.* I did not see God, I *did see* the heavens.

"I grew tall; but if I had not known my instructor, Sicard, my mind would not have grown as my body, for my mind was very poor; in growing up *I should have thought the heavens were God.*"

His instructor records the following conversation with him at one time:—

"What were you thinking about while your father made you remain on your knees?"

"About the heavens."

"With what view did you address to it a prayer?"

"To make it descend at night to the earth, in order that the plants which I had planted might grow; and that the sick might be restored to health."

"Was it with ideas, words, or sentiments, that you composed your prayer?"

"It was the heart that made it. I did not yet know, either words, or their meaning, or value."

"What did you feel in your heart?"

"Joy, when I found that the plants and fruits grew; grief, when I saw their injury by the hail, and that my parents still remained sick."

The sick persons whom he wanted restored to health, were his parents. He went out many evenings, during his mother's illness, and prayed to a particular star, which he selected for its beauty, for her recovery. Finding that she grew worse, he became enraged, and threw stones at the star. His teacher said to him:—

"Is it possible that you menaced the heavens?"

"Yes."

"But from what motive?"

"Because I thought that I could not get at it to beat it, and kill it, for causing all these disasters, and not curing my parents."

That star was the cause of sickness and hail-storms, in his view. He supposed it to be the super-human being, who had power to frustrate the purposes of man.

He had no idea of the cause of the growth of animals and vegetation, other than the heavens coming down upon the earth. He became very curious to witness the remarkable phenomenon. Being asked, "Did you know who made the ox, the horse, etc.?"

"No; but I was curious to see them spring up. Often I went to hide myself in the dykes, to watch the heavens descending upon the earth, for the growth of beings. I wished much to see this."

Before he became acquainted with Sicard, he says, "I did not know whether I had been myself made, or whether I made myself."

Is not here a sad picture? A poor deaf boy, at thirteen years of age, has no correct idea of God, and those great truths that belong to his existence;

he does not know whether he was made, or made himself; he supposes that the heavens came down at night upon the earth to make animals and vegetation grow; and that a beautiful star sends hail to destroy the plants, and disease to afflict his parents. If his subsequent life did not prove that he possessed an acute mind, we should be disposed to think he was a simpleton. But such an idea is not admissible in his case; for he became what some would call a genius. As a specimen of his written answers to questions, while he was yet a youth under the tuition of Sicard, take the following: —

"What is hope?"

"Hope is the blossom of happiness."

"What is the difference between hope and desire?"

"Desire is a tree in leaf; hope is a tree in blossom; enjoyment is a tree in fruit."

"What is gratitude?"

"Gratitude is the memory of the heart."

"What is time?"

"A line that has two ends; a path that begins in the cradle and ends in the tomb."

"What is eternity?"

"A day without yesterday or to-morrow; a line that has no end."

"What is God?'

"The necessary Being; the sun of eternity; the mechanist of nature; the eye of justice; the watch-maker of the universe, the soul of the universe."

This is truly beautiful, and indicates a mind of superior grasp. It is what may be called picture language of the most pleasing character.

Sir James Mackintosh is said to have put to him the question: "Does God reason?" and the boy returned this remarkable answer: —

"Man reasons, because he doubts; he deliberates, he decides. God is omniscient; he never doubts; he, therefore, never reasons."

This is probably the best answer that was ever given to the above interrogative.

It may be said, perhaps, that the case of Massieu is a solitary one, and, on that account, proves nothing. True, if it were the only case of such melancholly darkness of mind on record, in the midst of intellectual and moral light, it would not prove much; but there are a multitude of similar examples to which to appeal. Indeed, in every instance where no special pains have been taken to instruct the deaf child, similar ignorance and degradation have been the result.

A deaf and dumb person, in an American Institution, was asked how he felt when he saw such a difference between himself and other folks. He replied: —

"I was much surprised at the speech of the folks, when I saw them speaking; I had much desire to speak and hear; *but thought that somebody had stolen my hearing when I was a young boy.*"

A deaf pupil in a school in Edinburgh, Scotland, said to his teacher: "Before I came to school, I thought that the stars were placed in the firmament like grates of fire; and that the moon at night was like a great furnace of fire. I did not know how the stars and moon were made; but I supposed that the people like us, above the firmament, kindled the moon and stars; and I did not know whether the stars and moon were made by art or not; I thought the world little and round, like a table, and was always intending to go to the end of it."

A lady who became a pupil in an American Asylum at a mature age, said, after she had been instructed, "that her friends had taken great pains to give her some idea of God, but all she had been able to comprehend was, that this name belonged to a number of strong men, living above the sky, who printed the Bible, and sent it to us. The idea that the world must have had a Creator, never occurred to her, nor to any other of several intelligent pupils of similar age, and of equal advantages for acquiring ideas of religious truths. One of them ascribed every change of the weather to her parents, and called upon them to make it agreeable to her wishes, and vented her passion upon them when disappointed."

The deaf and dumb pupil of Charlotte Elizabeth is another kindred example. He was about twelve years of age when he went to her, pointing towards the sun, with gestures, and asked if she made it? "I shook my head." — "Did my mother?" — "No." "Did Mr. Roe, or Mr. Shaw (the two Protestant clergymen), or the priest?" He had a sign to express each of these. "No." — "Then, what, what?" with a frown and stamp of fretful impatience. He was answered properly, and seemed partially satisfied. He said, "he did not know how the sun was made, for he could not keep his eyes on it; but the moon, he thought, was like a dumpling, and sent rolling over the tops of the trees, as he sent a marble across the table. As for the stars, they were cut out with a large pair of scissors, and stuck into the sky, with the end of the thumb."

One day, after he had been taught that God made the stars and all other things, he went to his teacher, under considerable excitement, and said, "he had looked every where for God: he had been down the street, over the bridge, into the church-yard, through the fields; had peeped into the grounds of the castle; walked past the barrack-yard; and got up in the night to look out of the window. All in vain; he could not find God. *He saw nobody big enough to put up his hand and stick the stars into the sky.* 'I was bad, my tongue must be pulled out; for there was God, NO!' And he repeated 'God, no' so often, that it went to my heart."

In the "Memories of the French Academy of Sciences," is recorded the case of a person who was deaf and dumb until he was twenty-four years of age. Suddenly, one day, when the bells of his native city were ringing, his sense of hearing was restored. He became an object of much interest in consequence; and the divines questioned him in relation to his ideas of God, of the human mind, and of good and evil. On these subjects they found him entirely ignorant. He had lived twenty-four years without acquiring any knowledge of the most important moral trnths. There was no God, no human accountability, no hereafter, no moral good or evil, to his vacant mind.

Here are examples enough to show that the case of Massieu is not a solitary one; that it belongs to a class, which is by no means small. It cannot be doubted, after reading these facts, that deafness is a greater barrier in the path of knowledge than blindness. We look in vain for any such sad illustrations of mental darkness in the annals of the blind. With the ears unsealed, it would be quite impossible to live twenty-four, or even thirteen years, without making considerable advancement in knowledge, though no direct effort were made to this end.

The case of Kitto differed from those narrated, in the fact that he did not lose the sense of hearing until he was twelve years of age. These twelve years of communication with the world, by the hearing of the ear, were of immense advantage to him after his ears were sealed. He had acquired much information, to serve him when he was compelled to journey on in silence. Correct knowledge of men and things, to a certain extent, had prepared him to surmount obstacles which otherwise might have completely hedged up his way. All this is granted. Still, the foregoing examples are in point, as showing that the loss of hearing is a worse affliction than the loss of sight, so far as the acquisition of knowledge is concerned. This barrier was thrown up in Kitto's path after he was twelve years of age. Not so great an obstacle, to be sure, as deafness from his cradle would have been; but, nevertheless, an obstacle which very few besides Kitto have surmounted.

CHAPTER XVI.

ONWARD AND UPWARD.

A view of the Pauper as a Scholar—A great change—The humblest youth may win the confidence of men—Studies hard and progressed rapidly—Reasons for his close application—(1.) Appreciated the kindness of his Benefactors—Extract from letters showing his gratitude—The ungrateful Youth assisted by Mr. Harvey—The Charity-Student who filled a Drunkard's Grave—Gratitude incites to Duty—(2.) He followed the advice of elders and superiors—Letter to Mr. Barnard—Many youth ruined by not heeding advice—Rev. Legh Richmond's eldest Son—Wrote Letters of Advice to himself—Illustrations—Kept in mind his humble origin—In this respect unlike Scaliger and Bandinilli—(3.) Devoted himself to study, with application seldom equalled—In bed six hours—Letter to Mr. Woolcombe—Pascal—Bunyan—Baxter—Franklin—Alexander Murrey, and his triumphs.

HAVING seen that Kitto encountered almost as great obstacles as possible in the path of knowledge, we now turn to trace his progress from the time he was admitted to the Public Library of Plymouth.

We behold him, a mere boy, a pauper, fresh from the almshouse, admitted to a room containing some twelve thousand volumes. Only a short time before he looked wistfully through the bookseller's shop-window, unable to gratify his thirst for knowledge beyond the purchase of penny and half-penny books. Now he stands in the midst of a more choice collection of books than he ever saw in the bookseller's store, with the delightful privilege of revelling among them to his heart's content. The reality opens before him like a scene of fairy land. Can it be that a penniless lad, so recently the child of hunger and wretchedness, is thus privileged beyond even the sons of titled dignitaries? Yes! for he has worked his way to the hearts of benevolent men, and now he reaps the advantage of cherished virtues and faithful endeavors. His case is an illustration of the fact that the humblest youth may so conduct himself as to secure the confidence and esteem of mankind. Many appear to think that their condition excludes them from the possibility of winning a place in the hearts of the honored. But so long as a work-house boy, to whose sad lot of poverty is added the still sadder experience of deafness, wins for himself the regard of the learned and good, such a sentiment must be declared untrue. The poet was right when he said:

> "Honor and shame from no condition rise;
> Act well your part, there all the honor lies."

Kitto at once devoted himself to reading and

study with untiring zeal. He did not allow a moment to run to waste; but, on the other hand, he studied to make the most of every day and hour. Several things contributed to this result.

In the first place, he appreciated the kindness and generosity of those who contributed to his advancement. A few extracts from his letters to different friends, will show that his gratitude was full and free.

He wrote to Mr. Barnard: "If I could ever forget, or cease to remember, with respectful gratitude, the name which you, sir, bear, I should be the basest, the meanest, and most ignoble of human beings. Never will that name be by me forgotten, till the heart on which it is engraven shall beat no longer, and the pulse of the hand with which I write to you shall no longer vibrate."

He wrote to Mr. Harvey: "True gratitude is very seldom eloquent, and never suffers itself to evaporate in words. If, therefore, I fail in expressing my sense of the favors I have received from you and the other gentlemen, it does not imply that I do not, as, believe me, sir, I do, feel grateful, with a gratitude which words are too poor to express; and which shall be displayed, not merely by letters formed by a quill, or by verbal eloquence, but by an earnest *endeavor* to profit by the means which you have placed within my reach; of improving my moral and intellectual powers; of maturing my judgment, and of acquiring information."

After having visited Mr. Harvey one day, he wrote as follows in his Journal: —

"I remained at his residence nearly two hours and a half, and he shook my hand with great cordiality on parting. I had well nigh forgotton to say that he incidentally mentioned a youth of rare native genius, whom he had warmly befriended, as it appears, but who, in the end, proved very ungrateful to him. Mr. Harvey must be a gentleman of an extremely liberal and philanthropic mind, or he would not, after having once been greatly injured by his patronage of an obscure individual, have run the risk of a similar mortification, by befriending me. What assurance had he that I, the inmate of a work-house, should not make an ungrateful return to him for the blessings he meditated conferring upon me? None in the world. And how highly, therefore, am I indebted to him for his zealous exertions in my behalf. If his object was to rescue from obscurity a name which, at a future period, might become eminent, he will, very probably, be disappointed, for celebrity I do not hope to obtain; but never shall he be disappointed by experiencing an ungrateful return from me for the numerous benefits I have received from him, and through his labors on my account. No! whatever else I may be, never will I merit the imputation of being ungrateful."

Such feelings towards his benefactor, prepared him to improve the opportunities kindly afforded him for mental culture. His gratitude was something more than mere declamation, and he determined that his actions should proclaim it as loudly as his words. It is unlike the spirit which many recipients of kindness have manifested. The author once knew a student, who was indebted to the generosity of friends for his education. He was a young man of superior abilities, and might have shone as a star of the first magnitude among the *literati* of the land. But he was one of the irresponsible class. No favor received appeared to awaken the least gratitude in his heart. The more he was aided, the more he expected aid. And for all these generous deeds, he returned only idleness and wasted time. He improved no opportunities for intellectual advancement, further than his instructors forced him to do. While he might have been the first scholar in his class, he became the poorest. Bad habits, even those of a vicious nature, gradually took possession of his heart, and he became dissipated. Aid, however, was continued until he was graduated at a New-England college. He went forth into the world, a lover of strong drink, a young man devoid of principle; and, in a few years, went down to a drunkard's grave.

If the proffered assistance of his benefactors had been appreciated by him, and such grateful emotions as Kitto expressed had been awakened in his heart, it is believed that his career would have taken a different turn. He needed this deep sense of obligation, this grateful recognition of indebtedness to others, in order to stimulate him to industry and perseverance in his studies. Without this gratitude any youthful beneficiary is liable to err from the path of rectitude.

In the next place, Kitto was solicitous to follow the advice of his elders and superiors. His letters abound in recognitions of the counsels of his friends in regard to his conduct and studies. Unlike many of his age, he appeared to feel that those who were wiser and more experienced, could lead him better than he could lead himself. He wrote to Mr. Barnard, who sent him a letter of good advice: —

"Even in this most pleasing period of my life, few things have given me greater satisfaction than the letter which I received two hours since from you. I know that I have no more zealous friend, or one more really anxious for my welfare, than yourself; and, therefore, I can never be so blind to my own interest, as to neglect to attend to your admonitions and advice, under whatever circumstances I may receive it. I consider it as an incalculable advantage that in you, at least, I shall have a friend who will, though perhaps with but a distant eye, watch over my safety; and, when he sees me exposed to dangers of which I may not be aware, will caution me to avoid the precipice, on the brink of which I may stand; and who, when he thinks me neglectful of my duty to God, and my fellow beings, will remind me that these duties must ever be paramount to every other consideration."

This is the spirit with which every youth should receive the advice of age and wisdom. There is no doubt that it contributed largely to the success of Kitto. It shielded him from dangers which otherwise might have proved his ruin, and enabled him to choose the path to usefulness and distinction.

How many youth refuse to be governed by the advice of their elders! They are self-confident, and *know* that they are fully qualified to direct their own steps. Even their parents are distrusted, and their tender counsels set aside as peculiarly whimsical and useless. On this account, society abounds in youthful folly and recklessness. Young men, and even boys, who thank nobody for advice, crowd the ways of sin and death. They are painful illustrations of human weakness, to be seen in every rural district, and especially in every populous city. That young man who left a happy home, and kind parents in the country for city life, and was ruined by the tempter in a few short months, — was he not counselled wisely? Ah, yes! The last words of his doting mother, as she smiled a blessing through her tears at parting, bade him take heed to his steps. And that father: did he not discourse faithfully upon the temptations of the city; the danger of tampering with the sparkling wine-cup, and the perils of the theatre? Alas, the good advice was all thrown away, as words without significance, and the young wayfarer soon fell among his destroyers! The world has many a sad and mournful tale of woe to relate, in consequence of contempt for wholesome counsel.

The eldest son of Rev. Legh Richmond, after having received the very best instruction at home, was sent away to school. He was the subject of much thought and solicitude, as well as many prayers. He left home with line upon line, and precept upon precept. Perhaps he then determined to follow the counsels of his parents; but he found a companion whose habits were loose, and whose morals were corrupt. Gradually he was drawn towards him, until their acquaintance ripened into the closest intimacy. His father's counsels were no longer regarded. He saw no need of being so careful and strict about his conduct. The good advice of home now appeared superfluous. He thought he could control himself better than his father. The result was that he went astray; and, in a few months, was a ruined boy. He was taken home, and finally, as a possible means of reclaiming him, he was sent away to sea. His morals did not improve, until sickness laid him low, and death stared him in the face. It is believed that he died a renewed young man.

There are thousands of youth and young men,

who are ruined every year, in consequence of thus disregarding good advice. He who treats proffered counsel thus lightly, is about sure to make shipwreck of his hopes.

That John Kitto understood very well what good advice is, is evident from the following extracts from some of his letters written to himself, in order to improve in the art of composition, and "give himself that advice which no other person could give him." He was in the habit of addressing letters to himself, as if penned by some kind and interested friend. From these letters we extract the following: —

"It will be unpardonable if you neglect to avail yourself of the opportunities which you now enjoy of acquiring that knowledge and information which you once wished to obtain. And yet, it will be nearly equally inexcusable if you destroy your health, and irreparably injure your constitution by too close an application to your studies."

"My opinion of your judgment would considerably decrease if I thought that you estimated your progress in the acquisition of knowledge by the number of books you read. Make not books your sole study; study *nature* also, that you may delineate her accurately in your works. Believe me that many can elicit more instruction from *one* book, attentively read, than mere superficial readers can from fifty. Reflection is a more necessary ingredeint in the composition of another's character than reading; and you can indulge in reflection as well, if not better, when the grand panorama of nature is spread out before you, than you can in a closet, or in a splendid room, wherein your prospect is bounded by four walls."

"Always remember the obligations you are under to those philanthropic and disinterested individuals who have thus provided for you; and do not imagine that you will retain their friendship longer than you continue to deserve it. Let not your present prosperity too highly elate you. Ever recollect your humble origin, and do not forget that some unexpected circumstance may again consign you to that poverty and wretchedness from which you have emerged."

"Enjoy the present: make the most of the opportunities you now possess, and leave the future to itself and to your friends. The present only is our own; both the past and the future are beyond our power; and it is, therefore, the mark of a little mind to suffer the fears of futurity, or regret for the past, to embitter our present moments, and to cool our exertions in the pursuits in which we are engaged."

It is truly noble for a youth to advise himself in this excellent way. He who does it sincerely, as Kitto did, scarcely needs the counsels of others. He possesses such discretion, and just views of things, as will be likely to preserve him from evil. He will not be rash, or foolish, in his plans and purposes of life.

One sentiment in these counsels to himself deserves particular notice. He instructs himself to "recollect his humble origin, and not to forget that some unexpected circumstance might again consign him to that poverty and wretchedness from which he had emerged." How many there are, both old and young, who wish to conceal their *humble origin!* Their pride is wounded if any allusion is made to the obscurity from which they have sprung. Even some men of distinction have endeavored to magnify their origin. Julius Cæsar Scaliger, who was a distinguished critic, was so mortified at being known as the son of a miniature painter, that he wrote a memoir of his own life, in which he attempted to prove that he was "the last surviving descendant of a princely house of Verona." Bandinelli, an Italian sculptor, who rose from poverty to affluence, changed his name on several occasions, in order to hide his obscure parentage. He finally selected the name by which he is generally known, in order to make it appear that he descended from an honored family. Such examples are not rare. History frequently records them. But we would speak of this sort of pride chiefly as it pertains to the young. Many youth, in the circumstances of Kitto, would have desired to forget their humble origin. They would not have it known that their parents were poor and obscure; and this false pride is the bane of their lives. It has ruined multitudes.

Not so with Kitto. He would remember that he was nursed in the lap of penury; that his childhood was familiar with hunger and nakedness. He would remember it for his own good; that he might be kept humble, and be stimulated to make better improvement of his intellectual advantages.

Again: he devoted himself to study, in his new position, with a zeal and determination seldom, if ever, surpassed. We have spoken of his studious habits before, but we refer to the subject again for the purpose of showing more definitely what his labor was.

Not long after he was admitted to the advantages of the public library, he wrote in his Journal: "I am seldom in bed before twelve o'clock. Resolved never to remain in it after six, if I can help it. Six hours sleep are sufficient for all purposes of nature; but of late, I have often been in bed full seven hours."

He wrote to Mr. Woolcombe: "Sometimes I am industrious enough, but generally I am too lazy, and cold, and sleepy, to stay up *later than twelve*, and not unfrequently I even get into bed before; now, however, the hands of my watch indicate the quarter to *one*, and I am neither lazy, sleepy, nor cold; but my aching head longs for the pillow, and I am going to indulge it."

Little can be said in favor of burning the midnight oil in poring over books; but the fact that he devoted so many hours each day to study, shows with what zeal he improved his privileges. It was with similar devotion to learning, that most of the distinguished scholars of the past won for themselves a name. It was this which enabled the gifted Pascal to pursue a brilliant career, though he was afflicted most of his life with a painful malady. It was this

18

which produced the "Pilgrim's Progress" in the jail of Bedford; and this which brought forth the "Saint's Rest," on a bed of extreme suffering. It was this entire consecration to their pursuit, almost turning night into day, that contributed to the success of Franklin, Newton, and a host of other worthies known to science.

It was only by such improvement of time that Alexander Murray rose from obscurity to renown. His father was a shepherd, having "no debts and no money," and Alexander was destined to follow the occupation of the father. When seven or eight years of age, he was sent to the hills with the sheep; but his eyes rested more upon the books that he carried with him, than they did upon the flock. A friend sent him to school for a while, and there he read all the books, pamphlets, and papers, which the scholars brought into school, never joining them in their sports, and usually reading long after his companions were asleep. In this way he became the distinguished master of several languages, and was finally appointed Professor of Oriental Languages in the University of Edinburgh.

Such things as we have named contributed to Kitto's onward and upward progress. Without these, his course might have been widely different. There were two sentiments, however, in addition to those referred to, which exerted a happy influence upon his life. We shall speak of them in the following chapter.

CHAPTER XVII.

TWO IMPORTANT IDEAS.

"He must make himself," was the first—Read lives of great men—Lines of Longfellow—Work, a condition of Life—The mass study to live easiest—The Idle Genius, and studious, though sluggish mind—Sir Isaac Newton—Daniel Webster—Thomas Scott, the Commentator, a remarkable example—Lines of a Poet—Patrick Henry—Usefulness, was the second idea that possessed his mind—Call upon the Quaker, and his advice—Few influenced by this motive—The strongest motive to fidelity—A New-England Clergyman.

EARLY in his literary career, Kitto says that he became impressed with two ideas which exerted a controlling influence over his life. The first was, to express it in a common and homely phrase, *he must make himself.* He had read the lives of distinguished men, and found in every instance, that each was the "artificer of his own fortunes." He saw there was no royal road to literary distinction, and that it was by constant application that the most gifted triumphed over difficulties in their path.

These were noble sentiments for him to imbibe, in the beginning of his eventful life. They are excellent ideas for any and every youth to embrace, whatever may be his chosen pursuit. So many entertain views of the opposite character, and which stultify their efforts for life, that even one example like that of Kitto is a matter of congratulation.

We have only to look around us, and become familiar with the motives that actuate the mass of youth, and even adults, to understand that few cherish this noble sentiment which fired the breast of Kitto. The aim appears to be, to live in the easiest manner possible. Instead of making work the great condition of life, they study to ascertain how they can soonest rise above the necessity of toil. Hence, many youth choose those vocations which promise affluence in the speediest manner. The marts of trade are thronged with this class; bright, ambitious youth and young men, anxious to be rich enough to live without work. Perhaps they are willing to work hard for a season, if they can by and by enjoy their ease in affluent circumstances. It is not surprising that so many make a failure of life, influenced as they are by this false idea. Failure is almost inevitable.

Occasionally we meet with a scholar, who entertains the same opinion with regard to learning. He considers himself a genius, perhaps; not obliged, like inferior minds, to work out his intellectual salvation. It will do well enough, he thinks, for dull scholars to study, study, study, but no such necessity is laid upon himself. The result is that his superior abilities lose all their lustre, and pupils of inferior parts outstrip him in the path of knowledge. We remember one such youth; the son of a talented clergyman. His father regarded him as unusually promising. Other people called him remarkably bright. He was so often told ofhis uncommon abilities, that he was led to regard himself a genius. When about fifteen years of age, he was sent away to school, accompanied by the son of a neighbor. His companion possessed a dull mind, and he had to work for whatever knowledge he acquired. Not so with our smart young friend. He could commit readily; and an ordinary lesson was disposed of in a few moments. On this account, he had many leisure moments, and they were spent in idleness. When counselled about his course, and advised to improve his time, he would reply: "There is no need of it; it will do well enough for E——— (his companion), to study all the time, but I can advance rapidly enough without doing it." The last we knew of these two youth was, that the dull companion had won honors in a New-England College, and entered upon his chosen profession with high promise, while the *genius* had utterly failed in the halls of learning, and had become a sailor. This is only one of many facts, which prove that *work* is a condition of success. There are no talents so exalted, as not to need the discipline of constant application. Sir Isaac Newton said, that his triumphs were won by "continued application." Daniel Webster also remarked, "that he knew of no superior quality he possessed, unless it was his power of application. To this, and not to genius, he owed his success."

Kitto was right, then, in supposing that he must make himself what he desired to be. Patronage could not do it. All the wealth in the world could not do it. The best mental faculties could not accomplish it without toil. His own undivided, earnest, self-denying efforts alone could secure the end. He was a sagacious youth to perceive the truth; he was a wise one, to reduce it to practice.

We have intimated that the life of almost every distinguished scholar is an illustration of the topic under discussion. We cannot dismiss it without citing one or two examples. Thomas Scott, the renowned commentator, was designed by his father for the medical profession. He was sent to school, where he contracted vicious habits, and was sent home in disgrace. His father was so disappointed and enraged, that he treated him with great severity; and, for nine successive years, made him a complete drudge. Young Scott had a taste for books, and it was frequently manifested during this period; but his father, as if to punish him for his boyish tricks at school, wholly opposed his inclination to study, and took away the books which he would read during the long evenings of winter. This exasperated Thomas, and he secretly resolved that he would one day gratify his literary taste. He continued, however, in his old pursuit of grazier, until one day, his father censured him unjustly and severely. He immediately cast off his laboring apparel, informed his father that he should henceforth take care of himself, and started from home. His mind was made up, it had been for some time, he would be a minister. Without money or friends, he applied himself to study; and in due time expressed his desire to the proper ecclesiastical authorities, to be ordained. But his first effort to gain ordination was unsuccessful. Some young men would have been disheartened in his circumstances; but the disappointment appeared to call his energies into exercise with renewed strength. He had determined to occupy a certain position, and occupy it he would. He would work for it to the very last. He says, " I went again to reside at Boston, where I applied dilligently to my studies; but I was greatly frowned on by many of my relations; and I frequently heard the laugh of the boys, as I walked about the street in a brown coat, and with lank hair, pointing me out as the 'parson.'" He heeded them not; but determined that he would yet occupy a position where respect, and not ridicule, would be his portion. Every day he advanced. "He set his face forward, and all the appalling forms of discouragement could not divert him. Victory over one enemy gave him additional power to attack another." The result is known to the world. Wherever the English language is spoken, and the English Bible known, there the name of THOMAS SCOTT is familiar as a household word. But he achieved his own fortune; he made himself what he was. His life was an illustration of the lines: —

"Here's a lesson all should heed,
Try, try, try again.
If at first you don't succeed,
Try, try, try again.

Let your courage well appear;
If you only persevere,
You will conquer, never fear;
Try, try, try again.

"Twice or thrice though you should fail,
Try, try, try again.
If at last you would prevail,
Try, try, try again.
When you strive, its no disgrace,
Though you fail to win the race;
Bravely, then, in such a case,
Try, try, try again.

"Let the thing be e'er so hard,
Try, try, try again.
Time will bring the sure reward;
Try, try, try again.
That which other folks can do,
Why, with patience, may not you?
All that 's *been* done, *you* may do,
If you will but try again!"

Patrick Henry made several unsuccessful attempts to do business of different kinds. His failure was so complete that his relatives and friends despaired of his ever doing anything. Mortified by his failures, he resolved within himself to rise to eminence. He applied himself to the study of the law with little prospect of success, in the view of friends. But he entered upon his studies with the determination to *work* out his destiny. The whole man was roused. "Where there is a will there is a way," seemed to be the soul of every act. In a short time he was admitted to the bar. He continued to study and improve. Month after month he toiled on, and the more his mind labored, the more he was resolved to triumph. About this time, a controversy with the clergy arose in Virginia, which we have not space to detail. Suffice to say that an important case connected therewith, came into court, and Patrick Henry was retained as counsel on one side. When he arose in his turn to address the jury, there was little prospect that he would win the case. Popular sympathy was with the other side. He was exceedingly awkward, too, in his exordium, and stammered it out in a very unpleasant way. But soon a change came over him. His eye began to flash; his face glowed with interest and deep emotion; his form became erect, and he poured forth a strain of eloquence almost unequalled. He carried with him jury and court, and won the case most triumphantly. No sooner was the case decided, than he was taken up by the crowd, and borne away upon their shoulders, amid thundering shouts of applause. It is another illustration of the rewards of personal exertion.

The other important idea which early possessed the mind of Kitto was that USEFULNESS ought to be the great aim of his life. It was impressed upon his mind in the following manner. We let him relate it in his own words:—

"In a very early stage of my history, a gentleman of my native place, a member of the Society of Friends, invited me to his house, and sent me away laden with books; and with counsels which I then thought, and now think, the most valuable and quickening which I ever received. His grand point was this,—that it was the duty of every rational creature to devote whatever talents God had given him to useful purposes; to aim at the largest usefulness of which he might be capable; and that so far as I did this, and abstained from rendering the good gifts of God ministrant to the idle vanities of life, so far might I expect his blessing upon the studious pursuits to which I seemed inclined, and which had hitherto done me much honor.

"With much good taste and forbearance he refrained from urging upon my notice his particular views of usefulness, but left me to apply the general principle he had laid down. And I did apply it. When the reader reflects how arduous the task was to bring myself into a condition of usefulness, he will not wonder that the hope of usefulness to others had never before occurred to me. The idea seemed too mighty for me, and I could not at first grasp it. It oppressed me, by seeming to lay upon me the burden of duties and obligations which I had not previously contemplated; and yet it pleased me to trace the conviction, in the mind of the speaker, that I was not inevitably doomed by my affliction, to an unprofitable and useless life, but had become, or might become, subject to the high responsibilities which his words described. For many years these words haunted me like an internal voice, and became a sort of conscience to me; and I became happy or not, in proportion as I supposed the objects which engaged my solicitude were, or were not, involved in the large views which had been placed before me. I owe much to this. It opened my mind to a new range of ideas and influences; and my experience affords no more striking illustration of the wise man's saying, 'A word spoken in season, how good it is.'"

It is very evident that if USEFULNESS is made the leading principle of action, every faculty will be disciplined, and every opportunity improved in the best possible manner. The youth who is actuated by this high and generous purpose, is conscious of acting wisely. The noblest part of his nature is developed, and he commends himself to the esteem of all observers. God looks down upon his efforts with approbation, and he labors on, cheered by a happy conscience, and the smiles of a benignant Providence.

Yet how few are controlled by this important idea! How few plan and execute with this noble end in view! Among the young, how very small the number whose aim is so high and honorable! Other considerations, too often of a selfish nature — perhaps fame, wealth, or honor — move them to strenuous exertions. The purpose of life is thus belittled. Their souls are rendered sordid, ever grovelling in the dust of earth; and they make men and women of selfish views and hearts.

There is no doubt that a sense of obligation respecting this subject of usefulness, will enable a person to make sacrifices under hardships, and surmount obstacles which otherwise would dishearten and stop him in his course. There is now in the ministry of New England, a talented divine, who commenced his preparatory course of studies after he was twenty-one years of age. He was a carpenter by trade, and thought not of entering the ministry until he was converted in early manhood. He was entirely destitute of means, and without a friend who could render him any assistance. But a sense of duty impelled him to decide for the ministry. He did not dare refuse the command which seemed to fall upon his ear from the skies. He began to study, working a part of the time each day at his trade. Months passed by, and his improvement was very marked. He was early at his work in the morning, and late at his studies at night. He subjected himself to a system of the most rigid economy. Sometimes he boarded himself for a season, as Dr. Franklin did, in order to save means to prosecute his studies. His wardrobe was reduced to the smallest possible expense, without causing him to appear uncivilized. If he was under the necessity of going to any place on business, he took his book in hand, and walked the whole distance, studying as he went. In this way he prepared himself for college, and entered. To defray his expenses there, he taught school in the winter season, and, at other times, sawed wood for the professors and students, and did such other things as would add to his pecuniary means. He was graduated with high honors, and few ministers have ranked higher in point of ability, and few have been so much beloved as he. It was a desire to render himself useful to his fellow-men which begat and fostered his literary taste. Without this sense of obligation to mankind, he would not have begun a course of study. But this, becoming the leading principle of life, carried him through trials and difficulties, to the glorious consummation of his hopes.

The operation of the principle, then, was not unusual in John Kitto. If it was one of the elements of his great success, its effect was no more than what it has been in every breast, which it has animated with hope and zeal.

CHAPTER XVIII.

DENTIST AND PRINTER.

Sent to learn the art of Dentistry—Why?—Offer of Mr. Groves—Kitto's feelings about it—Attachment to Mr. Groves—Progress—Hints about his becoming a Missionary—Sent to Islington, to learn the art of Printing—His secret dissatisfaction—Little time to study—Pocket-Reading—Roger Sherman—Nathaniel Bowditch—Ten minutes a day saved—A thousand people save the time of thirteen students.

THE announcement that Kitto subsequently became both dentist and printer, may somewhat surprise the reader. He will instantly inquire, if he so soon relinquished his literary pursuits for the mechanic arts. Did his love of change lead him to try different pursuits, and illustrate the old maxim, "a jack at all trades, and good for none?" By no means. The sequel will show that he acted by the advice of the gentlemen who associated themselves to be his guardians, thus illustrating the topic upon which we have dwelt; viz., his willingness and desire to be counselled. They believed it would promote his highest improvement to engage a portion of the time in some mechanical pursuit. On this account, they made arrangements with a Mr. Groves, of Exeter, a dentist, and a gentleman of unsullied character, to receive John into his family, allowing him all his time for literary pursuits, except four or five hours in a day, in which he would learn the art of dentistry.

It should be stated that this arrangement was a benevolent offer on the part of Mr. Groves, who had become acquainted with Kitto's condition and promise. He offered not only to receive him as a gratuitous pupil, but, in consideration of any services he might render, to allow him, in addition to board and lodging, fifteen pounds the first year, and twenty pounds the second, promising to increase it to a permanent salary, if he should remain beyond that time.

This offer was very unexpected to Kitto, and it elicited expressions of profound gratitude from his pen. He accepted the proposal, and wrote a characteristic letter to Mr. Groves, from which we extract the following: —

"The external goods of life cannot be undervalued by one who once possessed very few of them indeed. I have, therefore, always been desirous of having some more certain dependence than the precarious fruits of authorship. In consequence of this desire, few things could give me equal pleasure to that which I derived from Mr. Lampen's, and your own communication, and if gratitude can be shown by a zealous endeavor to give satisfaction, and to peform my duties, you will not, sir, be long in discerning how grateful I am.

"With the arrangements which you mention, I cannot but be completely satisfied. It is more than I could be entitled either to hope for or expect, and I am afraid that my poor services will very inadequately compensate for your liberality.

"Thanking Mrs. Groves and you, sir, for your kind wishes for my welfare, I remain her and your very obliged and obedient servant,

"J. KITTO."

Early the following month, Kitto left his native town to reside with his new benefactor at Exeter. In Mr. Groves he found a friend, kind and watchful as a father. His heart was at once drawn to him, and mutual interest and affection ever characterized them thereafter. On this account, he was happy in his new position. He keenly felt the separation from his friends at Plymouth; but the kindnesses and privileges of his new abode caused him to be contented.

How did he like the work of a dentist? Did he

acquire a knowledge of the art? Thus inquires the reader. We are enabled to give a favorable answer to both of these interrogatives. In a letter to a friend, he wrote: —

"The business of a dentist is of a very various nature. *The employment is agreeable.* It does not occupy *me* more than, on an average, five hours daily; and my part of it, as yet, consists in the formation of artificial teeth, not from ivory, but a harder substance, the tusks of certain foreign animals."

He applied himself to the acquirement of the art with the same earnestness that he did to every thing else, and he rapidly advanced. When he had been at Exeter nearly a year, Mr. Groves made such arrangements for missionary service, as would bring his own labors as a dentist, to a close, in a few months. He proposed to Kitto to commence the practice of dentistry at Plymouth, having an office of his own, after he (Mr. Groves) had retired. The proposition was favorably entertained, as Kitto had then no intention of relinquishing the business. The subject was dismissed, however, for the present, as the time of Mr. Groves' departure was some months distant. This arrangement, in which many of the people of Plymouth were much interested, speaks well for the progress of Kitto in his new employment. That such a lover of books, who was covetous of his time for literary purposes, should so readily acquire a knowledge of this art, is indeed remarkable. It was the fruit of certain qualities we have named, in connection with some that remain to be discussed

About this time, some of Kitto's friends began to think of his becoming a MISSIONARY. In certain circles it was the subject of frequent conversation; and, indeed, his own attention was called to it. Whether it was in consequence of this, and with special reference to this result, or not, that Mr. Groves subsequently suggested his removal to the Missionary College at Islington, to learn the art of printing, we do not know; but on learning that more printers were needed at several of the stations of the Church Missionary Society, it occurred to him that Kitto might acquire the art, and thereby enlarge his sphere of usefulness, on some field of missionary labor.

The proposition was made to Kitto, after consultation of his friends, and he submitted himself to their decision. They decided that he should go to Islington to acquaint himself with printing, and he went. This new situation proved uncongenial to him in one particular; viz., it consumed nearly all his time, so that he had little opportunity for reading. This was a great trial to him; perhaps the sorest trial he had experienced since he left the work-house. But he submitted without uttering a complaint, because it was the opinion of his friends, that this was a judicious plan. The printing office was in London, two miles from the Missionary College, and he was obliged to walk this distance early every morning, and return late in the evening. Hence, the principal time he could get for reading and study, was after eight or nine o'clock in the evening. From what has been already said of his literary taste and habits, the reader will infer that he made late hours for learning's sake. Such was the fact. Although he usually returned wearied and jaded by the labors of the day, yet he seldom failed to devote two or three hours to his books. This fragment of time, which he wrested from the hours of sleep, served to cheer him somewhat in this position.

There was another way of progressing in knowledge, which he adopted at this time, and it deserves particular attention. While he was obliged to be at the printing office through the day, it frequently happened, that he found considerable time there.

There were always fragments of time which he could snatch from business in the course of the day, and devote to reading; and sometimes there would be several hours when he had no work. He was just the youth to redeem those moments from utter waste, and make them yield the highest possible pleasure and profit to himself. He was wont, therefore, to fill his pockets with books in the morning, that his mind might have work when his hands found nothing to do. He never went to the printing office without carrying one or more books in his pocket; and he never passed a day there without finding more or less time to read. In this particular, his life was a complete transcript of that of Dr. Franklin, who added something to his knowledge every day by improving the moments in which he was not setting type.

At this point we discover the secret of many person's success. The art of improving the smallest portions of leisure time has been carried by some people to perfection. Roger Sherman always took a volume with him to his shoemaker's bench, and there was no day when he did not find a few moments to read. The same was true of Nathaniel Bowditch. Poverty compelled him to work while it was day; but his book was always on his shoe bench, so that he could catch it up occasionally, and read for a moment. It is surprising how much a student may accomplish in this way alone; by mere pocket reading. Even if he finds but ten minutes in a day to read, he can advance a little. And who cannot find as much time as this? Where is the youth or adult who can truthfully say — I cannot find ten minutes in a day to read. There is time enough wasted in every neighborhood, by idle moments, to result in general diffusion of knowledge therein, if it were carefully redeemed, and devoted to intellectual improvement. Behold the multitude of persons of all ages, who trifle away their evenings at places of general resort, such as stores and depots, besides wasting many minutes in the day by lounging, or in useless conversation and jesting. The same persons will complain, perhaps, that they have no time for reading. Let them once possess the spirit of Kitto, and make an economical use of time, and there will be no ground for this complaint. If twelve persons in a community redeem ten minutes each in a day for reading, two hours will be saved to that community. If one hundred individuals do the same, more than sixteen hours will be saved. If the entire population, say a thousand people, do this, then *one hundred and sixty-six hours* will be gained each day for mental culture. In a single year of three hundred days, this would amount to almost *fifty thousand hours*, or more than *four thousand days* of twelve hours each, in the aggregate. Divide and distribute this time, and it would furnish thirteen persons with *three hundred days each year* for study! So much time saved by a community of a thousand people! Equal to the whole working time of thirteen students! And every town or village of a thousand people might redeem this amount of time as well as not; for they waste far more than this every year. How much this would do towards a general diffusion of knowledge among the people!

CHAPTER XIX.

BIRTHDAYS.

Learning character from manner of spending Birthdays—The multitude make them occasions of sport—Kitto's views of the subject, and his practice—His Grandmother celebrated his Birthdays with candy—He asked for Books—What he wrote about it when nineteen years old—A Birthday Letter to Rev. Mr. Lampen—It shows he was a remarkable youth—That he had sterling worth—That he was blessed with forethought and foresight—Accustomed to form just views—Was conscientious—Had moral and religious principle.

MUCH may be learned of a person's character from the views he entertains of his birthdays, and the manner he spends them. A little observation with reference to this subject, will satisfy the reader of the truth of this remark. He will discover, especially among the young, a tendency to devote these anniversaries to sport and pleasure. They are usually considered fit occasions for mirth and hilarity. Parties of pleasure assemble to celebrate them. The more worldly-minded and trifling the youth, the more he is disposed to make himself merry over his passing years.

As the views and practice of Kitto, in this regard,

differed somewhat from those of youth generally, it is important to consider them here. If we recur to some items of his experience in childhood, when he dwelt with his grandmother Picken, we shall find that some importance was attached to his birthday. They were celebrated, in a small way, by a supply of sugar-stick, and other confectionery, and pleasant strolls abroad. But as the boy advanced in years, he began to ask for books on these occasions, in the place of candy. He finally succeeded in obtaining the present of a little book of his grandmother at these times, instead of the usual supply of cake or sweet-meats. Thereafter, his birthday was celebrated in an intellectual way; he sought to please his mind, and not his palate.

At nineteen years of age, he wrote as follows upon this subject: — "There are two ways of commemorating the return of that period (birthday); the one *sensible*, the other *intellectual*, which do not always coalesce. There may be the commemorating feast, the dance and song, while the heart is full of sadness. The real and most essential, appears to be the private and intellectual. The external should correspond with the internal act; but if it did, would not the voice of condolence on this day be more frequently heard than that of congratulation? Would not festive mirth, and the outward signs of gladness, be frequently discarded for the garments of desolation, sorrow, and mourning?"

Kitto was in the habit of distinguishing each birthday by addressing a letter to some one of his friends, or penning one to himself from a fictitious correspondent. The following letter, addressed to Rev. Mr. Sampen on his twentieth birthday, will exhibit his views and feelings upon this subject more clearly than any statements of ours: —

"EXETER, December 4, 1824.

"REV. AND DEAR SIR, — For two or three years past it has been my custom to write a reflecting and anticipatory letter on the anniversaries of my birthday. The two last were addressed to a being who possessed no name or local habitation, nor any properties but those with which my imagination had clothed him. But, having for the present renounced the pleasures of a correspondence with this fictitious personage, I beg leave to take the liberty of devoting a short space of the evening on which I complete the twentieth year of my existence, to you, although the *subject* which the occasion suggests is too trite and common to afford a compensation for the time spent in the perusal of anything that can be written on it. Nevertheless, since uniformity is not a characteristic in any class of human minds, and, since the circumstances of external being, and the modifications of ideas and feelings are so astonishingly varied, I should hardly think the triteness of a subject a sufficient reason for declining its consideration. Whatever else may be uncertain, this much, at least, is certain, that the reflex operations of my own mind on such occasions, although frequently unpleasant, have never been to me void of interest, or unprofitable. Of anticipations I cannot speak so favorably, because they so seldom keep within the bounds of that devoted submission which Christianity demands of its professors, and because the domains of anticipation and castle-building are so interlaced that it is difficult to take a comfortable stroll in those of the former, without danger of intruding on those of the latter. I wish, however, to be permitted to protest against being considered as thinking *all* anticipation to be useless and improper; for if I did so, my thoughts would scarcely be consistent with that character which is the summit of my ambition, and to which I most ardently aspire; for a Christian is almost necessarily an anticipator, but then, his anticipations relate to no improper objects.

"In point of round numbers, the completion of the twentieth year is a kind of epoch in human life; a period on arriving at which we can, seated as it were on an eminence, without taking in the details of inferior subdivisions, look generally back on our past experience, muse on its pains, its vexations, and its hopes, and estimate its aggregate value and amount. Let me, then, do this; let me summon the thoughts and actions of my life from infancy till now, before me, and inquire the result. They pass rapidly before me, and the impression they leave on my mind is general. In this review, the details are different, of course, from those Solomon has so eloquently expressed; but the conclusion is the same: 'Behold, all is vanity and vexation of spirit!' Twenty years! how long a period — perhaps, too, the most important period of life — and oh, to how little purpose, in reference to the most essential objects, has that long and important period been employed! I have, I believe, among others, what the world considers a good character; and whatever various opinions those who know me may have formed of my head, I believe they are nearly simultaneous in their appreciation of my heart; but assuredly, did they see me as God has seen me, and I see myself, and were they fully acquainted with the corruptions of that heart, they would regard me with detestation. I say this from none of those motives of affected humility, which seek the pleasure of being contradicted. I express my feelings, my decided convictions; but it may be that I express them with no very anxious desire of being beloved. . . . . During these twenty years God has been a very good and gracious father to me; and now I can acknowledge and discern his guiding and preserving hand in many circumstances which, when they occurred, I, in the foolishness of my heart, imagined to be cruel and unjust. . . . .

"That I may have room to say something of my anticipations, I must drop my reflections and proceed to these. 'Where am I likely to be on my next birthday?' is a question which, on such an occasion, seldom fails to occur to the mind. I answer it thus: Should I live, there is no strong probability of any alteration in my external circumstances in the interval; and if there should be, and if it should appear for the worse, still I hope that I shall be submissive to the will of Him who always wills and does that which is best for the ultimate good of his creatures. To the question of whether I may live or die, I never felt more indifferent than at this moment. I am persuaded that the days of my pilgrimage will not be much prolonged, and, perhaps, if I have a bias on either side the question, I rather wish they should not be so. But if in the designs of his Providence, God should see fit to render me an instrument of any degree of usefulness, however small, to his church and people, I should rejoice to live. Shall we now then see the sum of the whole matter? It is this: What I have been, and what I have done, I hope God of his great mercy will pardon and forgive; that what he has enabled me to be, he will improve and stregthen; that he will purify me from evil, and render me daily more comformable to his divine image; that whether my external circumstances be adverse or prosperous, or whether I live or die, *my* will may be subservient to his; and that I may feel the most absolute conviction that he does, and always has done, all things well."

What is the inference from the foregoing? What do such views of birthdays indicate, concerning the character of a young man? Such a case is unusual among the young, and, for that reason, it is more instructive. Contrast these serious and reasonable views of birthday anniversaries, with those of the great majority of youth who associate them only with frolic and utter worldliness, and what do they show respecting their possessor?

They are indicative of a sterling worth. They cause every reader to feel that such a youth belongs to no ordinary class; that he must possess elements of character of a high and promising order. How noble and manly are these substantial sentiments, in contrast with the frivolity of multitudes upon the same subject! How much more consistent with manhood, and those moral obligations which are devolved upon every member of the human family. It is certainly no occasion for frivolous words and acts, that another year of precious life has passed away; that we are one year nearer to the grave, and the stern realities of an untried world. It is no occasion for frolic to any one that he had lived another year in thoughtless indifference to the claims of God, and without any honest endeavor to do good, and glorify his Father in heaven. Yet the conduct of the young generally on these birthday occasions, seems to say, the rapid flight of time, and continuance in worldliness, is occasion for gladness. "Let us eat, drink, and be merry, for to-morrow we die."

Kitto's birthday letter shows that he had both forethought and foresight; that he was accustomed to form just views of things; that reflection, consideration, conscientiousness, moral and religious principles, were elements of his character. Hence the manner of his spending a birthday becomes an index of his heart. It reveals more clearly than much positive declaration, what were the real qualities he possessed.

CHAPTER XX.

FOUR OTHER QUALITIES.

Singleness of Purpose—Determined to be a Scholar—Never lost sight of the object when Shoemaker, Dentist and Printer—Thomas Simpson—Thoroughness—Did all things as well he could, whether reading a book or mending a shoe—Method—How he studied History—How divided his time—Interesting diagram—Elihu Burritt—A Member of Congress—Independence—Want of it ruins many youth—Mansfield—Letter of Mr. Woolcombe to him about it—His views about a Memoir of himself—Wanted to *be*, not *seem*—Made him prompt—Napoleon—Conclusion.

WE have hitherto considered a number of Kitto's qualities, which may be regarded as elements of his success; but there are four others to which we would call the reader's attention. They are readily derived from what has been already said of him.

The first is, singleness of purpose. By this we mean devotion to one grand, all-absorbing object, in distinction from a division of time and efforts among several. Many persons undertake several different pursuits in life, and excel in none. They go from one thing to another, with the hope of hitting upon something that will materially add to their prosperity. All the while, however, they only just live, simply because divided efforts run to waste. But Kitto's heart was set upon one thing. One object absorbed all his thoughts. He did not care particularly for anything else. That object was LEARNING. This he desired beyond all other earthly possessions. For it, he was willing to toil, and make almost any sacrifice. We speak now more particularly of the beginning of his course.

On one occasion, when he was entreating his father to take him from the Poor-house, and allow him to struggle for himself, with an education in view, he gave utterance to the following language, which shows that not only one high purpose animated his soul, but also an unconquerable spirit dwelt within his breast: "There is no fear of my starving in the midst of plenty. I know how to prevent hunger. The Hottentots subsist a long time on nothing but a little gum; they also, when hungry, tie a light ligature round them. Cannot I do so to? Or if you can get no pay, take me out without, and then I will sell my books and pawn my neckerchiefs, by which I shall be able to raise about twelve shillings; and with that I will make the tour of England. The hedges furnish blackberries, nuts, sloes, etc., and the fields turnips; a hayrick or barn will be an excellent bed. I will take pen, ink, and paper with me, and note down my observations as I go; a kind of sentimental tour; not so much a description of places as of men and manners, adventures, and feelings." A youth with such a purpose and spirit, does not often fail of success.

Look back upon that part of his life already sketched, and see if you can find a period when he lost sight of this one object. In the work-house he was a shoemaker; but was he not still a self-denying, laborious student? Can we not trace his determination to acquire knowledge, even when he was most zealously employed at his trade? In like manner, when his friends decided that he should acquaint himself with the art of dentistry, was he not still earnest for a thorough education? Was it not equally so when he was a printer? While he devoted himself to these pursuits with an ardor worthy of all commendation, his heart did not lose a jot of its love of knowledge. Underneath all the interest he manifested for the manual labor his friends desired him to perform, we discover a strong, irresistable current of feeling, setting towards the fields of literature and science. Whatever else he might be temporarily, to please his benefactors, he was determined to be a learned man eventually. It was this one noble purpose that animated his soul amid all his trials and disappointments. It gave him courage when otherwise he would have faltered in his wearisome way, and developed an energy and perseverance which defied the stoutest opposition.

His example, in this particular, was like that of Thomas Simpson, a well-known scholar, who flourished some more than a hundred years ago. This latter personage, was the son of a weaver, so extremely poor that he could not allow his son but a few weeks schooling. After he had been in school just long enough to learn to read, and acquire a taste for learning, his father took him out, and set him to work at a loom. But the boy's desire for knowledge could not be quenched, and he eagerly read every book he could get. His father sternly rebuked him for what he considered his bad propensity, and forbade his looking into a book. But Thomas resolved within his heart that he would one day be a scholar. From that moment, he never lost sight of his object. In consequence of his propensity to study, his father turned him out of the house, and forbade his return. Although penniless and homeless, he did not yield to discouragement. He was still strong in the resolution to become a scholar. He secured lodgings in the family of a widow, and paid his board by working a portion of his time at his trade. When not toiling at his trade, he was poring over his books. Subsequently, he was tossed about, as men say, "from pillar to post;" but he still resolved in his heart to acquire an education. No disappointment or privation caused him to flinch one iota from his original purpose. If pressure of circumstances compelled him to turn aside for a while to other pursuits, it was only to obtain the means of securing the one great object of his life. The result is briefly told. He became a distinguished mathematician, and was appointed Professor of Mathematics at Woolwich, when he was only thirty-three years of age. He published several of the most elaborate mathematical works extant. From beginning to end, he was actuated by a single purpose.

Another quality of Kitto was THOROUGHNESS. When the young are obliged to devote themselves to a calling in which they are not interested, their advancement is usually slow, if they advance at all. It is a kind of drudgery to them; and therefore they apply themselves only just so far as they are compelled to this end. The same might have been expected of Kitto. Ardently attached to books as he was, and resolutely determined to have an education, it would have been rather natural for him to slight his work, and prove a very superficial toiler. But such was not the case. *Thoroughness* was an element of his character, so that whatever he did was well done, whether it was reading a book, or making a shoe, or artificial tooth. At the work-house, he excelled all the boys in making list shoes. For this reason, a shoemaker selected him from the whole number, for his apprentice. In dentistry, his proficiency was so marked that, in a single year, it was proposed that he should set up that business in his native town. As a printer, he was no less thorough. Indeed, everything to which he applied himself, was speedily mastered. This made him a critical scholar. All the works which he published are impressed with this characteristic of his mind — thoroughness.

Another quality which contributed to his success, as it always does wherever it exists, was METHOD. This enabled him to husband his time, so as to make the most of each day. His attention was first called to the subject by reading the remarks of some writer thereon. They seemed to him important, and he at once applied them to practice. He was methodical, both in his division of time, and investigation of topics. The following is a description of his plan of studying history : —

" In studying history, when I commence the study, I shall use the following method: Geography of the portion of whose history I am about to read. The history, such biographies as exist of the eminent characters mentioned in the history. The principal existing works, if they can be obtained, of the philosophers, orators, and literary persons, who lived in the country, and during the period which the history embraces. This plan is only to be used in the study of ancient history ; in that of the modern, it would require to be greatly modified."

He promised to furnish Mr. Harvey with his plan of study, after he was admitted to the Public Library, " that he might be able to tell where he was, and what he was doing, at any time of the day or week. The following is an extract from his note to Mr. Harvey, containing the plan : —

PUBLIC LIBRARY, Aug. 7, 1823.

. . . . . "I have read so much of method, and the great advantages which occur to the literary student from the observance of it, that I long ago resolved within myself to make a systematic division of my time as soon as I should have it in my power. I have it now in my power; for, when on Tuesday, I casually mentioned my want of a watch to Mr. Hawker, he went and procured me one. The plan I have resolved on is as follows: *—

	MORN.	A. M.	P. M.	EVE.	NIGHT.
Sunday.	Red. 1	Brown. 2	Brown.	Brown.	Pink. 3
Monday.	Yellow. 4	Yellow.	Pink.	Pink.	Pink.
Tuesday.	Red.	Yellow.	Pink.	Pink.	Pink.
Wednesday.	Green. 5	Yellow.	Green.	Green.	Pink.
Thursday.	Yellow.	Yellow.	Pink.	Pink.	Pink.
Friday.	Red.	Yellow.	Blue. 6	Blue.	Pink.
Saturday.	Yellow.	Yellow.	Pink.	Red.	Pink.
Sunday.	Red.	Scarlet.	Red.	Red.	Pink.
	to 8 o'cl'k.	9 to 1.	2 to 5.	6 to 9.	10 to 12.

1. Optional. 2. Writing to Mr. Woolcombe. 3. Reading. 4. Grammar. 5. Writing to Mr. Harvey. 6. Extracting. 7. Church.

" Those portions of time which I have reserved to be used optionally, will be occupied in reading, writing, or walking, as circumstances may dictate or

*In the original diagram, the spaces are actually distinguished by the *colors*, of which only the names are here given.

permit. I shall spend all the time I possibly can in the library, rather than at my lodgings; but when not at the library I shall be at Mr. Barnards, unless I take a walk during one of the optional periods."

Later in life, he carried his systematic way of doing things into the arrangement of his library. So much order was observed there, that he could lay his hand upon any book he wanted in the dark. He allowed no person but Mrs. Kitto to touch an article therein, until his eldest daughter arrived to an age that rendered her generally useful, when the care of the room was transferred to her. She received written directions how to proceed, and these were often characteristic of the man. The following will serve as a specimen: —

"Plan, Programme, Protocol, Synopsis, and Conspectus, for cleaning Dr. Kitto's Table.

"1. Make one pile of religious books. 2. Another of books not religious. 3. Another of letters. 4. Another of written papers other than letters. 5. Another of printed papers. 6. Put these piles upon the floor. 7. The table being now clear, dust, scrub, rub, and scour until you sweat; and when you have sweated half a gallon, give over, and put the piles upon the table, leaving to Dr. K. the final distribution.

"Signed, sealed, and delivered, this twenty-eighth day of May, in the year of our Lord eighteen hundred and fifty-two.

"JOHN KITTO.

"*Witness*, HOLOFERNES PIPS."

This systematic division of time must have been of great value to him. The testimony of every successful student, and of every person distinguished in the trades and professions is, that method is indispensible to success. Many a man now living can bear witness that such system has enabled him to accomplish what otherwise he could not have done. Elihu Burritt, the learned blacksmith, belongs to this class. For years, he was wont to work at his trade a certain number of hours each day, while he devoted the remainder of the time to literary pursuits. By pursuing this plan he mastered a large number of languages while he followed his trade. A distinguished United States Senator, now in the vigor of his manhood, elevated himself from the cobbler's bench to his present position, by improving his time in the same way. He labored at his trade so many hours per day, while he read and studied the remaining time. Among other things, this method contributed, no doubt, to his rapid improvement.

Still another quality, which contributed to the success of Kitto, was INDEPENDENCE. We mean by this something different from obstinacy, or persevering recklessness. It is that quality which enables a person to rely upon his own manhood and principles, instead of pinning his faith to the sleeve of another, or truckling to public opinion. The want of this leads to untold evils in all departments of human effort. Those youth who yield to the wiles of the tempter, and take the intoxicating cup, or resort to gaming saloons, are generally destitute of this trait. A resolute, well-meant, determined "NO," would have saved multitudes of them from ruin. But they have not sufficient independence to utter this little word. An acquaintance invites them to take a glass, or play a game, and perhaps they at first decline; but they cannot hold out against much urging, so they yield to the pressing friendship, and go down, down, down to shame. True independence would lead them to utter a determined "NO," and declare plainly and fearlessly that they are principled against such wrong. When the celebrated Mansfield was attacked and threatened by a mob, on account of his course in a certain case which he tried, he said, "I wish *popularity;* but it is that which *follows,* not that which is run after; it is that popularity which, sooner or later, never fails to do justice to the pursuits of *noble ends by noble means.* I will not do that which my conscience tells me is wrong, upon this occasion, to gain the huzzas of thousands, or the daily praise of all the papers which come from the press. I will not avow doing that which *I think is right,* though it should draw on me the whole artillery of libels—all that falsehood and malice can invent, or the credulity of a deluded populace can swallow. I can say, with a great magistrate upon an occasion, and under circumstances not unlike, 'I was always of opinion that reproach acquired by well-doing, was no reproach, but an honor.'" That was independence, such as makes signal triumphs in the world. No matter what the pursuit of a person is, nor how humble his condition, this element of character elevates him.

Kitto was as much distinguished among his friends for *independence,* as for other qualities named. Mr. Woolcombe once wrote to him, "I most earnestly hope and entreat that you will ever preserve that independence of mind and character *which you pos-*

sess now. I know how difficult it is to maintain it. I see how few do preserve it, and I am aware that sometimes, great sacrifices must be made to retain it. I cannot trust, therefore, to professions; but nothing will tend more to secure my friendship, than to see that you practice it; not in a captious or offensive way, but in a mild, firm, decisive one."

This helped him to shun vicious courses; made him a critical thinker, and enabled him to form his own opinions of men and things. Perhaps it appeared in no respect more striking than in his own views upon certain subjects. He never embraced an idea because some other person advocated it, but only because it commended itself to his understanding.

Just before his departure for Malta, Mr. Harvey requested him to furnish the materials for a memoir of himself. Kitto's reply exhibits his independence of character in a good degree. We make a single extract: —

"In any future publication by myself, or concerning myself, it is my desire to appear fully as I am; and that it should be fully recognized throughout, *whose* I am, and whom I serve, I do not wish, or expect, all men to think and feel exactly as I do; but surely I have a right to hold, and express my own thoughts and feelings. I am fully aware that I hold some opinions which some will disapprove, and which will procure for me the stigma of being fanatical and enthusiastic. These *you* would, and *I* would not, wish to conceal. In short, I should wish most decidedly, that it should be a publication, so far as *I am concerned*, of a decidedly religious character; and not only so, but of *my own religion*."

While he ever submitted to the advice of his benefactors, he, nevertheless, had a mind of his own about every subject. Sometimes he expressed his differing opinions plainly, though in a modest, becoming manner. He did not always agree with his benfactors about the wisdom of their plans for his welfare. On several occasions he gave utterance to his non-agreement. At the same time he stated the ground of his opinion; and the results of his eventful life proved that he was right.

It was this trait of character which always made him so prompt. Resolution was always followed by immediate execution. The undecided person is ever delaying. He is fearing this and that, or waiting for some one to move, or something else to transpire. Perhaps he has to stop and inquire what public opinion is. "What will Mr. A say?" "Will Mr. B think well of it?" The noble independence of Kitto raised him above these perplexities, and therefore left no opportunity for delay. He determined, then executed. Once settled that he must be a barber, a shoemaker, a dentist, or printer, and he became such quicker than any one with whom he toiled. He was like Napoleon in this regard. This famous general owed much of his success to that independence of mind which made him the man for great emergencies. He looked over the field, took a bird's-eye view of his prospect, reckoned upon his chances, and then resolved. His camp was all astir at once; and, ere the foe dreamed that he was nigh, he charged upon them with all his force.

Which of the four qualities now enumerated was most valuable to Kitto, it is impossible to say. All of them were important, and no one of them could have been left out without producing a marked defect of character. They happily blended together in his successful career.

CHAPTER XXI.

A MISSIONARY.

Sailed for Malta—His early views of ministerial and missionary life—Letter to Mr. Flindell—Arrival at Malta—His immediate privations—How he liked his work—Letter to Mr. Woolcombe—Pledge to forsake literary labor—Reproved for immoderate study—Disconnects himself from the Mission—Review of the course of his benefactors—Not surprising that Kitto was aggrieved—His noble conduct under the trial—Meets Mr. Groves in London—Resolves to join his Mission to Bagdad—Ready in three days—The Journey—His trials greater than at Malta—The plague—In Bagdad three and a half years—Return to England.

ON the twentieth day of June, 1827, Kitto sailed for Malta, in company with Dr. Korch, a German physician, who had lately taken orders in the Anglican Church, and Mr. Jadownicky, a converted Polish Jew, just arrived from the United States, where he had been educated. He was appointed lay missionary by the Church Missionary Society, and went out with the design of making himself useful in his trade of a printer, and of rendering such other service to the cause of Christ as he might be able.

It is probable that Kitto would have become a minister but for his deafness. For at one time he appears to have been greatly elated at the idea, as it was suggested to him; and he wrote as follows:

"*Apropos* of Kirk White; I learn that his deafness was one of the reasons which induced him to relinquish the study of the law for the clerical profession. Till I had learned this, I had understood that a defect of hearing was an insurmountable bar to entering into holy orders. Were it possible, O my God! that I could become a minister of thy Word; that I could be permitted to point out to erring sinners the path of peace and salvation, what more could I desire of thee? . . . . How truly happy should I be in some retired and obscure curacy, where I should have no other business but the delightful one of instructing others in their duty to God, and their fellow-men!"

For a long time he had cherished the most exalted views of a missionary life; but had scarcely dreamed that he could render any service to the Lord in this noble way. When his attention was first called to the subject, more than three years before, he wrote to Mr. Flindell as follows:—

"Ever since I have been capable of forming an opinion upon any subject, I have always regarded with reverence those illustrious men, who, fired with apostolic zeal, and, unappalled by the probabilities of difficulty and danger, have left their friends and their country in order to promulgate the Gospel of mercy and truth in far distant countries; in lands pervaded by religious darkness, and sunk into intellectual degradation. What glory, what dignity equals that attached to the character of an ambassador of God? What triumph can be so noble and so pure as that of him who is enabled to exclaim, 'I have awakened a sinner to repentance; I have turned an idolater to the true God; I have been instrumental in saving a soul from death?'

"To me there appears to be something exceedingly grand in the very name of *Missionary*. Jesus Christ was a missionary, so were his Apostles; and so likewise were many of the ancient fathers. . . . .

"Even considering the character of a missionary abstracted from its utility and importance, it is still nearly identified with my *beau ideal* of human perfection. The missionary is the true Christian philosopher, and not the self-denying ascetic, who imagines that he does God service by the practice of rigid austerities, without being in any degree useful to his fellow creatures. From whom is he a missionary? From God. To whom, and why? To men plunged in the lowest depths of ignorance and stupefaction. He goes to them as the deputed messenger of God, to convert them from the worship of idols, and to lead them to that merciful and unkown Saviour who suffered for them, bled for them, and died for their sakes. Had the missionary a less important object in view than this, the resolution and zeal with which he pursued it, in spite of every impediment and affliction, would still give him the highest claim to our admiration and respect.

"To be a missionary requires capabilities of no common order. He should possess unshaken fortitude and patience; great sweetness of temper; unwearied industry; a zeal the most ardent and energetic, and a great facility in the acquirement of languages. 'The harvest is very great, but the laborers are few;' and never shall my feeble voice, while I live, cease to be added to that of others in entreating the Almighty to raise up skillful laborers to this great harvest, and in soliciting the blessing of heaven on missionary labors.

"Entertaining so exalted an idea of the missionary character, I doubted whether you, sir, were serious when you asked, 'Might not Kitto make a useful missionary, if he studied with effect the only book of sound principles and perfect science ever written?' But whether, sir, you were serious or not, you *certainly did not at the moment recollect the deprivation under which I labor of one of my external senses; a deprivation which contracts my sphere of probable usefulness within a very narrow compass indeed.* The book you mention is undoubtedly the Bible. That, sir, is a book which I have always delighted to study, and I hope that I have not studied it ineffectually. When I have been depressed it has raised me; it has consoled me when I have had no other consoler. Never, by me, shall this precious book be neglected; nor will I ever cease to study the divine precepts it inculcates."

The last paragraph of this somewhat lengthy extract shows that, while Kitto entertained the most ennobling views of the missionary life, he regarded his loss of hearing as an effectual barrier to success in that sacred calling. Then he did not think, probably, that he would ever be found doing service upon the missionary field. But Providence led him in a way he knew not.

Kitto reached Malta on the 30th day of July, and in due time was zealously engaged in the work for which he had been set apart. He met with many privations and hardships, and endured them as a Christian hero. He wrote to Mr. Harvey: —

"I found nothing on my arrival calculated to give me any expectation of much personal comfort in this place. I slept several weeks on the floor, and it was a considerable time before I had a chair and a table. I did not mind it, however, thinking as I did that it was not seemly for a missionary to complain of wanting this or the other articles of personal accommodation. I hope I had learned the necessity of being 'a man of few wants,' and therefore I did not trouble myself in the least about things which would have vexed me exceedingly, two years before."

He was not only contented in his new field of labor, but he really enjoyed it. With his accustomed, and even wonderful ability of adapting himself to existing circumstances, he engaged in his work with a zeal and relish quite surprising. He wrote to Mr. Woolcombe, after a residence of more than six months in Malta, and in his letter he says: —

"As a man and an Englishman, I should say,— 'nothing like home after all.' But as a missionary and a Christian, I feel that the place in which I am, is the best for me; for I am now really aware of no other, in which I could hope to be equally useful, and therefore I love Malta; but I have not felt that any feeling of this kind renders it necessary that I should love my own country less than I have ever done, and, I hope, ever shall do."

The same self-denying and noble spirit pervades his letters to Mr. Barnard. In one of them he writes: "I desire to be very thankful that circumstances were so ordered that I should remain in the Society's service. The situation of a missionary, whether lay or clerical, and under whatever circumstances, cannot fail to be a highly privileged and happy one, when undertaken on right principles and feelings. I could speak a little on this point *experimentally*. It is easy to talk about missionary service when we are at home, or even when we are preparing at home for personal services in the cause, and yet understand very little of what it really is. In this, as in other things, an ounce of experimental knowledge is worth a pound of speculation or conjecture. Now I feel in my own case that, after all, I have made very considerable sacrifices for the service. Relatives, country, friends, are powerful detentions, and it requires no small effort, even in a missionary, to break from them, especially when, though it be possible, it is not very probable, that the voluntary exile will ever again revisit the land he ought to love better than any other on earth. Again, it will hardly be said that my prospects of temporal emolument, when with Mr. Groves, were not better than the temporal realities of my present situation. Believe me, it is not my wish to magnify any sacrifice I may have been enabled to make; far from it. I only mention this that I might say how the consolations of Christ do abound in these situations, notwithstanding the difficulties and sacrifices with which they must be obtained. In my own case, I feel that my most ordinary employments, even my daily occupations, are, with the blessing of God's spirit, calculated to be the means of great usefulness to the Christian cause. This is what few but those in our situation, can say of their most *ordinary* duties."

When Kitto received his appointment as missionary to Malta, he pledged himself to relinquish literary pursuits, at least, so far as not to interfere with his work in the printing office. Accordingly, he industriously toiled at the office during the eight or nine hours it was open in a day; and then, regarding the remainder of the time as his own, he mainly devoted them to intellectual pursuits. He studied, of course, with his accustomed devotion, and made long days and short nights. A mind like his must have about so much nutriment in a day, to keep it from hungering and thirsting after knowledge.

On recovering from a severe attack of sickness, some less than two years after he entered upon his missionary work, he learned that the Committee of the Church Missionary Society were displeased with the manner he spent his time out of the printing office. They reasoned that such immoderate study must impair his physical health; and thus interfere with the faithful discharge of his obligations to the Society. Not long after he became acquainted with this fact, he received a communication from the Committee, forwarded by Mr. Bickersteth, who took occasion to say: "You are aware our first principles as christians, are the sacrifice of self-will and self-gratification; if you can rise to this, and steadily pursue your work, as you engaged to do, you may yet fill a most important station, and glorify our great Master. But if you cannot do this, it is clear that the Society cannot continue in its service those who will not devote themselves to their engagements." Kitto was much aggrieved by this communication, and at once took measures to disconnect himself from the mission. On the twelfth day of January, 1827, he sailed for England, having been in Malta less than two years.

The reader may justly wonder at the course pursued by the friends of Kitto, in regard to his wellfare. Did they not remove him from the work-house for the purpose of placing him where he could enjoy the advantages of mental culture? This was their professed object. They avowed it in their circular to the public. For a season, they gave him access to the Public Library. Here his intellectual advantages were great. He appreciated and improved them. But what then? These friends decided that he should acquire the art of dentistry. This was not so bad, however, since only five hours in a day were employed in this mechanical art, and this might promote his health and thereby facilitate his studies. But the next move was enough to crush the hopes of an aspiring student — the trade of a printer, without scarcely an hour for study, which was not stolen from the time for sleep. How can this be reconciled with the published intention of placing him in "a situation more consistent with his feelings and abilities?" And then, to cap the climax, he is sent away as a missionary to Malta, *pledged to forsake* literary pursuits, as the Committee say. Setting up type, in the publication of tracts and books for the benighted, without even the privilege which any mechanic enjoys, to spend his evenings in reading. Such requirements might be necessary for the Church Missionary Society; but how could the professed benefactors of Kitto consent to have him placed in these circumstances, when they proclaimed that they sought his mental improvement?

Who can blame Kitto for feeling aggrieved? For one, we frankly confess that we never read a more painful case of literary oppression. The boy was taken from the work-house that he might have time to study. He so understood it, and high hopes were raised in his heart. Grateful for what he considered the kindness of benefactors, he yielded always to their advice with the confiding nature of a little child; and lo, he soon found himself where his literary advantages were fewer than they were in the work-house! What student, thirsting for knowledge, would not be disheartened and grieved by such a result? How discouraging to one who is ever cheered on by the hope of one day walking unrestrained in the fields of learning! There is no part of Kitto's life which impresses us more with the excellent qualities of his heart, than his conduct under such unexpected treatment. For some time he felt that his friends were not acting for his highest good, and yet he submitted to their counsels and decisions. His acquiescence was always so seemingly hearty, that his own views to the contrary are not discoverable, except in two or three letters which he wrote. He seems to have reasoned, "I may be mistaken after all; my benefactors are men of wisdom, and they must know. I am young and inexperienced, and doubtless my judgment errs. I must, and will abide by their counsels." A noble spirit! But the sequel will show that the judgment of the boy was sounder than that of his friends.

After Kitto returned to England, he resolved to follow his literary inclinations; and two or three plans were suggested by which to shape his future course. He finally decided to superintend a private printing press, which employment would pay his way, while he pursued his studies. But before he entered upon this business, he met with Mr. Groves in London. The latter gentleman was on the eve of his departure as missionary to Bagdad. During their conversation, Mr. Groves said to Kitto, without scarcely expecting that the question would be taken in earnest, "Will *you* come?" To his surprise,

Kitto replied, without a moments hesitation, "YES." That brief answer determined his course for life. From that moment he entered upon a series of labors which were intimately connected with those achievements, that crowned his life with glory. Mr. Groves told him that, in a temporal point of view, he would be the loser; that he would sacrifice an honorable, and comparatively lucrative situation for one where he would enjoy neither. But Kitto was not daunted by these prospects of trial, and in three days he was ready to go.

Mr. Grove's party consisted of nine persons. They were nearly six months on their journey to Bagdad, every moment of which was enjoyed by Kitto. He always had a desire to travel, and become acquainted with persons and places, and this journey afforded him an excellent opportunity. Their safe arrival at Bagdad drew forth expressions of profound gratitude from our young traveller, and indeed, the whole party gratefully acknowledged the hand of God in their guidance and preservation.

In some particulars, Kitto's share of trials in this missionary field was greater than it was at Malta. It was during his residence at Bagdad that the plague visited that city. The mission did not escape, and two or three of their number fell victims to the terrible scourge. In a letter to Rev. John Marsh, Kitto says: —

"When the calamity increased, when four or five thousand died in a day, the people seemed to relinquish in despair, the endeavor to bury their dead. They cast them into the river, and Mr. Groves saw great numbers of dead bodies floating down the stream. Those who died in the streets, were left there unburied, and the horrid spectacle was presented, of bodies lying about, half devoured by dogs. . . . . .

"The plague in London was not comparable to this. There the weekly mortality, perhaps, never exceeded seven thousand. Here it had been nearly that in two days. There, the total destruction from the plague did not exceed fifty thousand; here it is computed to exceed that number, while the population of the city does not, perhaps, amount to more than one-fifth that of London, at the time of the plague there. In short, it is supposed that not less than three-fourths of the population have been destroyed in the course of something less than two months."

Kitto passed through this fearful period with calm

trust in God. Never, perhaps, did the christian graces shine more conspicuously in his conduct than during the ravages of this pestilence. He remained in Bagdad, connnected with the mission, about three and a-half years. The subject of withdrawing from the mission was forced upon his mind, by two considerations. The first was what he regarded a limited field of usefulness; and the second, the prospect of doing more good as an author, with his pen. He compared his influence over the boys whom he had in charge, to instruct, with the multitude of persons who are reached by the writings of a successful author; and the more he compared the two relations, the more he desired to return to England, and devote himself to literary pursuits. Whatever may have been said of his decision, at the time, his life subsequently proved that God directed his steps.

In July, 1833, he reached London; having been nearly nine months returning. He immediately fixed his abode at Islington, where he made arrangements to lead a literary life, the results of which will appear in the following pages.

CHAPTER XXII.

PUBLICATIONS.

Literary engagements—Synopsis of labors—His marriage—Attention turned to authorship—"Uncle Oliver's Travels in Persia" —"Pictorial Bible"—"Pictorial History of Palestine"—"Cyclopædia of Biblical Literature"—"The Lost Senses"—"The Christian Traveller"—"Thoughts among Flowers"—"Gallery of Scripture Engravings"—"The Pictorial Sunday Book"—"Ancient and Modern Jerusalem"—"Journal of Sacred Literature" —"The Tabernacle and its Furniture"—"Daily Bible Illustrations"—"Scripture Lands"—"Land of Promise," and "Sunday Readings for Christian Families"—Studies sixteen hours a day —Sitting up nights—Alarm clock—Aid of his wife—Still a poor man—Contribution of friends and of the Queen—Authors usually poor—Defoe, Goldsmith, Boyce, Homer, Hazlitt—Remark of Madame Terein.

IMMEDIATELY after Kitto's return from Bagdad, he settled at Islington, where he entered into literary engagements suited to his tastes and habits. He was employed by the Society for the Diffusion of Useful Knowledge, to write for their "Penny Magazine," on the liberal terms of one pound eleven shillings per page, and to contribute to other works sufficiently to fill up his time. In a letter to Mr. Harvey he defines his duties as follows:— "For the "Penny Magazine," to write one original article weekly, of about three columns; to prepare two or three columns more from the contributions of correspondents, or from books; to read the first proofs; to register the suggestions of correspondents; to answer letters with real names and addresses; to bring contributions into a fitting shape, and to return useless articles. For "The Companion to the Newspaper," to prepare the Monthly Chronicle of Events, and to analize Parliamentary Papers. For the "Printing Machine," to prepare the Journal of Facts in Science, Education, Statistics, etc.; and for "The Companion to the Almanack," to prepare the Chronicle of the Sessions, the Parliamentary Abstracts, and the Register of Events. I dare say other incidental duties will arise that are not included in this enumeration. For all this, my original articles not being as before, a separate and uncertain account, I am to receive at the rate of sixteen pounds monhtly."

About three months after Kitto's return, he was united in marriage to a lady of great worth, who rendered him important service in his literary pursuits, as we shall see on another page.

In less than a year after he entered upon these permanent literary engagements, his attention was directed more particularly to the preparation of books. We referred in a former chapter, to a volume of essays which he published at twenty years of age, and which was well received by the public. At this time, however, he commenced a series of labors which have ever associated his name with those of the most distinguished authors.

He prepared "Uncle Oliver's Travels in Persia," in two volumes, in which the manners, customs, and habits, of the people were delineated for the young.

About the same time, he began the "Pictorial Bible," which has been extensively circulated throughout Christendom. It contained original notes, "chiefly explanatory, in connection with the engravings, on such passages connected with the History, Geography, Natural History, Literature, and Antiquities of the Sacred Scriptures, as require observation."

This was followed by the "Pictorial History of Palestine and the Holy Land," a work of great value to the student of sacred literature; and, indeed, to every lover of the Bible.

Next appeared his "Cyclopædia of Biblical Literature, a work almost wholly unlike any other in the

English language. It was received with great favor, and attained a popularity at once.. It was issued in two large volumes, of nearly two thousand pages.

We should have said that, about the time Kitto engaged particularly in these Biblical studies, a friend called his attention to a work much needed, upon the trials, achievements, and lives of the deaf, dumb and blind. This was kept continually before his mind, while he was pursuing his more important researches, and he collected much material for the same, in this incidental way. In 1845, the work appeared, bearing the title of "The Lost Senses." The reputation of it is deservedly high.

"The Christian Traveller," in three parts, was the title of another, which was prepared after the manner of the last mentioned.

"Thoughts Among Flowers," was the title of a little volume which he published in 1843. In the same year, appeared also, his "History of Palestine, from the Patriarchal Age to the Present Time."

Another popular work was, "Gallery of Scripture Engravings, Historical and Landscape; with descriptions, Historical, Geographical, and Critical;" in three great volumes This work was before him two years, while he was employed upon other productions part of the time.

His "Pictorial Sunday Book," was issued in 1845. It contained thirteen hundred engravings, an Atlas, and an Appendix, on the Geography of the Holy Land.

Between the years 1846 and 1849, the London Tract Society published his "Ancient and Modern Jerusalem," in serial numbers. These contained descriptions of the Court and People of Persia, and an elaborate account of the Tartar Tribes.

Between the years 1851 and 1853, he prepared the "Journal of Sacred Literature." It appeared in two series, both of which contained *eleven* volumes.

"The Tabernacle and its Furniture," was publised in 1849. At this time, also, his attention was turned to a work which has probably contributed more than any other to his fame. It was the "Daily Bible Illustrations," in a Morning and Evening Series. The Morning Series was published in 1851, consisting of four volumes, of more than four hundred pages each. The Evening Series did not appear until 1853. It had the same number of volumes as the former, and was no less valuable. This work was designed for the use of families; and it has been extensively circulated in this and other lands.

Between the appearance of the Morning and Evening series of the Bible Illustrations, a period of four years, he issued the following three volumes; viz., "Scripture Lands," described in a series of Historical, Geographical, and Topographical Sketches, and illustrated by a Biblical Atlas, a volume of nearly four hundred pages. The "Land of Promise," or a topographical description of the principal places in Palestine, and of the country eastward of the Jordan, containing about three hundred and fifty pages; and "Sunday Readings for Christian Families."

Some smaller productions, in the form of pamphlets, we have not enumerated. The reader should understand, that while Kitto was preparing these works for the press, he had considerable writing in addition to execute, in order to meet all his literary engagements.

Surely here is work enough for an intellectual giant to accomplish. Most of the aforesaid volumes must have been prepared by great outlay of time and research. No one destitute of Kitto's power of application and perseverance could have prepared them. Some idea of his excessive labors may be learned from a passage in one of his letters, where he refers to the Museum, whither he resorted to consult costly volumes: "The Museum day, under any circumstances, is but *six* hours long, whereas *mine* is *sixteen*." His biographer, Mr. Ryland, speaks of his habits in this regard, as follows: —

"At first he tried the hazardous plan of sitting up night after night; but nature asserted her claims. He often fell asleep during the earlier part of the night, and when, on waking, he discovered that he had not done what he intended, he would turn to his desk, where his anxious wife frequently found him vigorously pursuing his task, when he should have been in his bed. For sitting up late, he then resolved to substitute early rising, having twice exposed himself and his family to the risk of a conflagration by his nocturnal slumbers in the library. An alarm clock was placed at the bed's head, sufficiently near for its whir to arouse Mrs. Kitto, on whom it devolved to communicate the shock to her husband. This plan, however, did not always succeed; and occasionally night vigils were resorted to; but an attack of bronchitis gave an unwelcome, though timely warning, and early rising, enforced by his medical adviser, was again adopted; a bell, which could be rung by the watchman, taking the place and performing the office of an alarm. This early rising apparatus, however, did not get into complete working order till he removed to Manchester Terrace, Islington, where the drawing-room was completely fitted up with book-shelves, and an Arnott's stove. On being aroused from sleep, he went to his study, and, having, by the aid of a spirit-lamp, prepared himself a cup of tea, he continued to write till the rest of the family were ready for breakfast. After that he usually employed himself in his garden; he then dressed, for he was the reverse of slovenly in whatever regarded personal appearance, and went to his library till one o'clock, his dinner hour. The interval between dinner and tea was generally given to answering correspondents, and correcting proofs At five he came to the tea-table with a book in his hand, and read to Mrs. Kitto. On returning to his study, he worked at the desk till between nine and ten, and then read till eleven. Such was his laborious, undeviating course, till within three or four years of his death."

This passage exhibits, not only the continued studious habits of Kitto, but, also, his *methodical* way of doing things, of which we have already spoken.

We have said that his devoted wife rendered him important service while he was prosecuting these herculean labors. She was a woman of excellent mind and heart, and was most unreservedly devoted to her husband's happiness. For a time after their marriage she made no atttempt to assist him in his literary labors, and during this period she was quite unhappy. The idea of not being able to render him essential aid caused her, at times, to be almost wretched. It was not until she proposed to do something that would directly assist him in his studies, and actually engaged in so doing, that she was wholly satisfied. She says: "Daily we walked together to the British Museum; he, to attend to his duties relative to the 'Penny Magazine'; I, to collect such material as he required for future use. Thus we pursued our course together, until his more onerous engagements on the 'Pictorial Bible' rendered it necessary for him to sit at home and ply his pen assiduously, whilst I, day by day, went forth to collect from all the various authorities pointed out by him, such materials as he needed. Thus, through me, he managed to supply the deficiences of his own library, as it was then. For many years this was my employment; for, although his stock of books increased largely, there were always many not in his possession, from which he wished to cull, and ever afterwards my services were in active requisition; and he used jocularly to designate me as his *hod-man.* Thus, we in time became as perfectly assimilated as was possible under the circumstances, and I no longer repined; in fact I had abundant reason to be thankful, seeing I had now become essential where I most desired to be so. Indeed, so essential did I become, that he could never bear my absence from home, except when he sent me forth, and then always begged me to hasten my return; saying that I stood between him and fate, and that when I was absent he was constantly in alarm lest he might be interrupted. Thus all the socialities of out-door life have been entirely set aside. During the twenty-one years of our married life, I may say, in perfect truth, *that ten hours have not been spent separate from him in visits.*"

There are few examples of like conjugal fidelity on record. It is not usual even for wives to so far adapt themselves to existing circumstances as to make their husband's success the one, all-absorbing aim of their lives.

Notwithstanding the large number of volumes which Kitto wrote, and the extensive circulation they had, he was nevertheless, a poor man. What he wrote ought to have made him independently rich; but he did not write for money, and cared little for it beyond a comfortable subsistence; therefore, he was usually content to sell his manuscripts for enough to meet the existing necessities of himself and family.

At one time he occupied a dwelling which he was expecting would become his own. He had arranged matters to this end; but the unexpected failure of one of his publishers, frustrated his plans, and he was obliged to sell the house at a great sacrifice, and remove his family to Woking. In several instances, his friends raised an amount of money for him, by private subscription, just to relieve him for the time. Finally, they made an effort to secure an annual grant from the Queen, on account of his eminent public services. This effort was successful, and he received thereafter, one hundred pounds a year, from the Royal Civil List.

And yet, at one time, the impression was quite

general, that Kitto was getting rich. In a letter to Mr. Tracy, he refers to this impression, and says, "I heard last week that there is a general impression in the city, that I am a very rich man. I accept this as an acknowledgment, that one whose works have been so well received by the public, *ought* to be so. So I might have been, probably, if I had commenced my career with any capital to enable me to retain the copyrights of my own works."

It is not unusual for authors to be poor. Our firesides are cheered by the writings of men whose penury denied them the luxuries, and even the necessaries of life. Defoe was a writer of celebrity, and was the author of some two hundred books and pamphlets, yet he died insolvent. Samuel Boyce was a well known literary character of the last century; yet he was so indigent that his friend, Dr. Johnson, often solicited aid for him. It was said of Homer, "the blind old bard of Greece," that "his mouth was oftener filled with verses than with bread." Savage expired in the jail at Bristol, whither he was sent for a debt of *eight pounds.* The gifted William Hazlitt was poor all his days. On one occasion, he met a friend who inquired after his health and circumstances. "Both are bad," said Hazlitt. "You are aware of my difficulties; those dreadful bills; those bad accounts; but no human being knows *all*. I have carried a volcano in my bosom, up and down Paternoster Row, for a good two hours and a half. Even now I struggle, struggle mortally, to quench, to quell it; but I can't. Its pent up throes and agonies, I fear, will break out. Can you lend me a shilling? *I have been without food these two days.*" A few months after, Hazlitt lay upon his death-bed, his mind agitated by the pressure of want. When too feeble to pen a line himself, he dictated the following note to the above named friend: —

"Dear Sir, — I am at the last gasp. Pray send me a hundred pounds.

"Your, truly,

"WILLIAM HAZLITT."

When the money came, poor Hazlitt was in his coffin.

A multitude of similar examples might be cited, but it is unnecessary. It was the general poverty of authors which caused Madame Terein, to advise Marmontel, as follows: "Secure yourself a livelihood independent of literary success; and put into this lottery, only the overplus of your time; for, wo to him who depends only on his pen! Nothing is more casual. The man who makes shoes is sure of his wages; but the man who writes a book is never sure of anything."

There are some noble exceptions to the foregoing, especially in our day. We hear of copyrights being sold, occasionally, for five, ten, and twenty thousand dollars, and more. The sale of a single book has yielded an author, in a few instances, quite a fortune. But such examples are rare, and must be considered exceptions to the general rule. A large majority of authors, in all ages, have been poor.

CHAPTER XXIII.

IMPOSSIBILITIES.

Not a believer in Impossibilities—His life a proof—Many youth falter before difficulties—Case of Laura Bridgman—The student in Rutger's College—Prescott, the Historian—Use develops faculties—Two right hands—Rugendas—The deaf and blind—Facts concerning certain powers they acquire—Dr. Woodbridge—The German Lady distinguishing color of surfaces by her fingers—Saunderson—The Blind Penman—The blind traveller—The blind watchmaker—The blind tailor—These facts show what?—The Blind speculator in Boston.

KITTO wrote in his Eastern Journal, "I am not myself a believer in *impossibilities*." In a letter to a friend he said, also, "But I thought then, and think to this day, that all the fine stories about *natural ability*, etc., etc., are mere rigmarole, and that every man may, according to his *opportunities and industry*, render himself almost anything he wishes to become."

There is truth in this sentiment. His own life proves it. There could scarcely be a greater difference between two persons, than there was between the boy Kitto wading in Sutton-Pool, and the man Kitto preparing the most elaborate works on Biblical Science. Or, looking a little further along in his career, the poor deaf boy making list shoes in the work-house did not appear much like the accomplished author of the " Pictorial Bible," and " Daily Bible Illustrations." If *impossibilities* ever existed, popularly speaking, they must lie somewhere between the deaf pauper and the gifted master of Oriental learning. But he did not find them there. All things became possible to him. He advanced from step to step as if he never dreamed of failure.

It is probably true that many youth are deterred from making persevering endeavors for any particular object or attainment, by the imagined impossibilities before them. How many scholars shrink from undertaking, or grappling with a difficult problem in arithmetic, or some other lesson that tries their power of application and their perseverance. A comparatively trifling difficulty is sufficient to discourage many in their course. Some think that a liberal education would be a valuable acquisition, and at once commence the necessary studies; but a little experience with Greek roots and Latin idioms disheartens them, and they turn away from books to other employments. Yet the difficulties which they encounter are not to be compared with those which beset Kitto's path. Destroy their vision, or close up their ears, and add poverty and wretchedness to their earthly lot; and then require them to master the sciences, and become learned and useful; what would they say? As soon would they undertake to swim the Atlantic, or lift Gibralter, as to surmount such difficulties. They believe in impossibilities; and this very belief unfits them, in a measure, to undertake great enterprises. It requires one to believe with Kitto, that all reasonable things are possible, if he would triumphantly advance. He who believes that he *can* do a certain thing, has already half accomplished his object.

It is scarcely possible to estimate the difficulties that lie in the way of educating a girl like Laura Bridgman, who can neither hear, see, speak, nor smell. Those teachers who undertake such a task cannot be believers in impossibilities. Their pupil is almost entirely shut out from the world, dependent for communication with those around her upon the sense of touch. Who would think of teaching a child arithmetic, geography, and other branches, by appealing only to the sense of touch? Can a child be educated to *feel* its way through this world, acquiring knowledge of passing events, and recognizing the high moral duties of life? Impossible! multitudes would say. Yet the case of Laura Bridgman shows that even more than this has been accomplished. Her intellectual faculties have been so thoroughly educated that she will make even brilliant recitations in various studies, with her fingers. She has come to exhibit all the tastes and preferences for certain branches of knowledge which the young, who possess all the senses unimpaired, are wont to show. Even her wardrobe is a matter of great interest to her. She exhibits a particular fancy for ribbons and finery, as other girls of her age do, and usually shows a preference for those visitors who are most richly appareled. In short, from an isolated being, she has become one of the human family in sympathy, intelligence, communication, and perception. Her progress is truly wonderful, when we reflect that in childhood, "the darkness of the tomb was around her; no mother's smile called forth her answering smile, no father's voice taught her to imitate his sounds; they, brothers and sisters, were but forms of matter which resisted her touch; but which differed not from the funiture, save in warmth, and in the power of locomotion; and not even in these respects, from the dog and the cat."

A young student in Rutger's College lost his

sight entirely by too close application to study. He was an orphan, without pecuniary means to defray his expenses, and two sisters dependent upon him for support. Is it possible for a young man thus situated to prosecute his studies, and care for his devoted sisters? Thousands would be overwhelmed by the calamity, and declare that they could go no further. But young Nelson had the valiant spirit of Kitto in his breast, and misfortune seemed to arouse his soul to greater exertions than ever. He began to instruct his sisters in Latin and Greek, while they read his text books to him that he might commit their contents to memory. His progress was truly wonderful. He became the star of the college. One day he differed from the Professor as to the manner of rendering a sentence in Virgil. The Professor finally ruled that Nelson was wrong, and gave what he considered the true rendering. In respectful language, yet with the color mantling his cheek, he replied, as he turned his sightless orbs to his instructor, "Your reading would be right, sir, if the mark were a comma, but in my Heyne's edition it is a colon."

He took his degree, and went forth to earn bread for himself and sisters. He was eminently successful, and his fame as a scholar spread far and near. He was soon made Professor in the college where he was graduated, and he won an enviable reputation in the office. He probably did more than any other man of his time, to elevate the standard of classical scholarship in our seminaries of learning.

Some years ago, a young man in college lost one of his eyes by a missile thrown by a class-mate. He was then seventeen years of age. The other eye became so affected by sympathy that its sight was endangered. The best occulists were employed, but to no purpose. He was sent to Europe, with the hope of finding relief, and for three years he tarried in that country. At length he returned with only part of an eye, just enough vision to serve him in travelling about, but too little to enable him to read. His father was an eminent jurist, and designed his son for the bar; but this great calamity so far blighted his hopes, that he turned away from the legal profession, to the less popular sphere of authorship. He decided to devote himself to historical literature. He spent ten years of laborious systematic study of the standard authors, before he selected his theme. Then he sat down to the stupendous undertaking, before which ordinary resolution would have vanished.

"Archives are to be searched; masses of manuscripts, official documents, correspondence, etc., are to be canvassed; old chronicles to be consulted; reading without end to be done, and notes without end to be taken." What a discouraging work for one who must read through the eyes of others! Yet it is done, though another ten years was demanded to perform the task. When Prescott was forty years old, his "Ferdinand and Isabella" was given to the public. And who does not know its fame? This has been followed by his "Mexico," "Peru," and "Phillip the Second," eleven large volumes of historical literature, which have justly earned him the reputation of a profound historian, on both sides of the Atlantic.

Such examples of persevering labor class well with that of Kitto, in showing that faith, patience, resolution and perseverance, can conquer apparent impossibilities. Surely, if young men under such privations, and almost unparalleled difficulties, can succeed in their chosen profession, there is little excuse for the failure of those, who, having eyes, see, and having ears, hear.

It is almost surprising to see how much can be accomplised by concentrated effort in one direction.

There is no doubt that any one of our powers of body and mind might be rendered far more acute and efficient by more thorough discipline. Hence, God has wisely ordered that loss sustained by the deprivations of one faculty may be supplied by increased acuteness and strength imparted to another. Thus persons who have been deprived of the use of the hands have learned to write and paint with the toes. Others have learned to use the left hand as readily as the right. This was true of the celebrated painter, Rugendas. He was first an engraver; but a weakness of the right hand forced him to resort to the lighter art of painting. The weakness of his hand continued to increase, however, until he could not use it at all. He was thus compelled to employ his left hand in the execution of pictures; and, in process of time, this would perform the work as successfully as the right hand. This proves that there is no reason for having both a right and left hand except *use.* We might just as well have two right hands, if we would only subject them to the proper discipline.

The same is true of the intellectual faculties. If we desire one of them to be particularly developed, we must tax it more. Its exertions must be systematic, earnest, and continuous. In this way, the blind, who are dependent upon others reading, soon become distinguished for tenacious memories. In like manner the deaf, who are deprived of hearing the living voice, often acquire the ablity of understanding a public speaker by the movement of his lips. Being thrown more entirely upon their own resources, those resources are developed, even to the surprise of the possessors.

Perhaps if John Kitto had not lost his sense of hearing, he might have continued to work as a stonemason to this day, without exhibiting more talent than was absolutely required to prosecute his business. But the loss of hearing shut him out from the world, and compelled him to retire within himself and *think*. Physical disability found its compensation in mental exercise and enjoyment.

Consider for a moment, some facts concerning the unfortunate deaf, dumb, and blind persons, of some of whom we have spoken, facts relating to the topic in question. Dr. Woodbridge was able, a few years after his sight was lost, to read the directions on a guide board, a full half mile off. Laura Bridgman can distinguish strangers from acquintances by the sense of touch, while she easily tells one acquaintance from another in the same way. Dr. Howe says, "When Laura is walking through a passageway, with her hands spread before her, she knows instantly, every one she meets, and passes them with a sign of recognition." From this it appears that she can recognize her school-mates without even touching them. A blind German lady, by the name of Paradisi, is said to have been able to determine the color of surfaces and the delineations on playing cards, by the use of her fingers. Saunderson could form a very good idea of the dimensions of a room, by the sound of his foot-fall on the floor. In the same way he could distinguish a tree from a post, at the distance of five yards; and a fence from a house, at the distance of fifteen or twenty yards. An English lady, who was deaf, dumb, and blind, is said to have excelled in the art of penmanship, and in some difficult patterns of needle work. Phillip Davis was a blind traveller of some note; and he thus gives his impressions of Dublin, on his first visit to that city:—

"Upon the whole, this place is rather a desirable situation; but its contrasts are greater than any I have found in all my travels; some of its streets possessing all the gaiety and opulence for which the heart of man can wish, while others exhibit all the wretchedness and want that the imagination is capable of forming. In this place, my ear was frequently saluted by the creaking boot of the opulent, mixed with the sound, on the same pavement, of the naked foot of the indigent."

He could discern the rich from the poor, generally, by the sound of their feet upon the pavement.

Blind William Huntley never saw the light; his calamity was born with him. He was brought up at the trade of watch and clock maker, in which he became distinguished. He would often succeed in repairing a clock or watch, where others failed in the attempt. The family tailor of an English gentleman, became blind fifteen years before his death. He continued to work, however, at his trade, and it was during this period that he made a Tartan dress, a very difficult piece of work, "because every stripe and color, of which there are often many, must fit to each other at the seams with mathematical exactness; hence it is that very few tailors, even in the enjoyment of vision, are equal to the task."

These facts show that individuals often acquire remarkable power in one direction, by discipline. Taxing one of the senses, or mental faculties, and continuing the process day after day, increase its ability ten-fold. This ought to teach us an important lesson in regard to general improvement. Application, perseverance in well directed effort, and industry uninterrupted, are sufficient to develope abilities for work that would otherwise become an impossibility. If a given amount of dicipline will render one faculty remarkably acute or strong, then it may another; and then, too, discipline enough may be commanded to unfold the powers of the whole man with equal prominence. Hence, a person can make himself, as Kitto says, "almost any thing he wishes to become."

We close this chapter with the account of a blind young man of our acquaintance. At the age of about ten years, the pupil of one eye was pierced with the point of a knife. The consequence of the accident was the entire loss of vision. At the time, there was nothing in his character or conduct which indicated particular taste for learning, or for any one of the fine arts. But he was necessarily obliged to retire within himself, and reflect. This gave a new impulse and direction to his mind. He was sent to the Blind Asylum at South Boston, where he made rapid progress in his studies. Without considering the details of his life, it is sufficient for our purpose to state that he became a successful teacher of music, and, for several years, has given instruction on the piano, harp, and several other instruments. He has also mastered two or three modern languages, so far as to be well qualified to give lessons in them. Nor is this the most remarkable part of his history. His judgment, discretion, and circumspection, appeared to develope rapidly after his mental faculties became so much stimulated. He conceived the idea of buying and selling real estate: one of the last things we should suppose a blind man would attempt. This was in the city of Boston, where he was a teacher of music. Certain dwelling houses were for sale, and he concluded that the buyer thereof might realize considerable profit. He consulted his father about the matter, who endeavored to dissuade him from what he regarded a wild project. It seemed to him almost utter recklessness, for a blind young man, especially one who was not reared in the sphere of traffic, to undertake speculation in Boston real estate. But the son reviewed the enterprise, and was more than ever convinced that it was a golden opportunity for money-making. He resolved to buy. He did buy, and made *five thousand dollars* by the purchase. He has effected other purchases and sales since, and is now worth some twelve or fifteen thousand dollars.

It is not difficult to trace the secret of his success. Those faculties, which have been so remarkably developed, were necessarily taxed more, after the loss of vision. He might not have become either a musician or a linguist, if blindness had not overtaken him. Neither might his judgment and circumspection, necessary characteristics of a good trader, have been so marked, but for that reflection which must have been occasioned by his dire misfortune. The fact shows how much can be accomplished when our faculties are thoroughly disciplined.

CHAPTER XXIV.

THREE MORE EXAMPLES.

The same elements of character lead to similar results—Blind Nicholas Saunderson—Could speak and write Greek and Latin—Professor at Cambridge—Blind Francis Huber—Became a distinguished naturalist—Singular discoveries—James Holman, the blind traveller—Travelled around the World—Described objects accurately—Told bust of Alexander, by touch—Governor of Tobolsk—Ascended to the main-topmast-head of a ship—Hunted elephants—Managed his own finances—Lesson from these facts.

EXAMPLES of eminent success among those deprived of one or more of the senses, have been cited hitherto, showing that elements of character like those possessed by Kitto, always lead to similar results. If Kitto's were a solitary case, we could not infer from it that certain qualities will triumph over great difficulties; but since there are many of similar nature, our conclusions therefrom may be correct and just. On this account, it may be well to cite two or three remarkable examples, in addition to the foregoing.

Nicholas Saunderson was born in the village of Thurston, Berkshire, in 1682. Before he was a year old, he lost both eyes by a severe attack of small-pox.

Though his father was a poor man, he resolved to give his son the opportunity of acquiring an education, as soon as he was old enough to be sent to school. Accordingly, at an early age, he was placed in the free school at Penniston, where his rapid advancement astonished both his teachers and fellow pupils. From the rudiments of knowledge, he advanced to the higher branches of study. He soon mastered the Greek and Latin languages, so that he could speak and write them almost as readily as he could English. He was able to follow persons who read these languages to him, catching the meaning of every word, as if he were listening to his own mother tongue. When it is remembered that he mastered these languages by having them read to him by others, his progress is truly wonderful.

But the poverty of his father compelled him to take Nicholas out of school, to his no small regret. Two neighbors, however, competent to the task proposed, offered to instruct him in algebra and geometry. He soon acquired all his teachers were able to impart, proving that his capacity for the science of numbers was even greater than it was for the languages. After this, he pursued his studies at home, by the aid of a reader.

At the age of twenty-three, a fellow of Christ's College succeeded in introducing him into that institution. Lodgings, and free access to the library, were tendered him. Several members of the college kindly contributed the use of their eyes, so that he was well supplied with readers. Here he was happy, and his improvement was marked. He was appointed to deliver a course of lectures in the college, upon the Loss of Sight: the last topic we should suppose a blind man would undertake to master. His lectures were very popular, and added much to his reputation. Six years from that time, he was appointed Professor of Mathematics at Cambridge; an office that was filled a few years before by Sir Isaac Newton. Here he was equally successful, and his fame brought many students to the university. It is said that he frequently went out in the evening with his pupils to make observations of the heavenly bodies, and that he would tell as readily as any one, when a cloud obscured a star. During the term of his professorship, he wrote and published several valuable mathematical treatises.

His literary career was one of splendor; and he went down to the grave, just past the noon of life, honored and mourned by all who knew him.

Francis Huber, the distinguished naturalist, lost his vision at seventeen years of age. Strange as it may seem, he devoted himself to the study of bees, making experiments and observations to ascertain their habits, and settle some questions which had perplexed naturalists. For instance, the origin of the wax was a subject upon which naturalists had written much, and different and conflicting theories had been advanced. Some had asserted that the bee manufactured it from the honey; but Huber succeeded in showing that "it escaped, in a luminated form, from between the rings of the abdomen." He thoroughly investigated the manner of their building their store-houses, and discovered that certain classes of bees did certain work. He instituted inquiries concerning the "locality and history of the bees' senses." He discovered how they ventilated their hives; and that they consumed oxygen, like other animals. Indeed, naturalists since his day have added very little that is valuable to the history of the bee.

Huber was a man of cheerful and happy disposition, and his sweetness of temper won him a large circle of sympathizing and confiding friends. On the twentieth of December, 1831, he wrote to an acquaintance, "Resignation and serenity are blessings which have not been refused;" and, on the twenty-second, he expired, at the good old age of eighty-one.

In 1811, a Lieutenant in the Royal British Navy lost his sight on the coast of Africa. His name was James Holman, the person to whom we made a passing allusion in another place. At the time of the accident, he was twenty-five years of age. He had seen somewhat of the world, of course, and cherished a strong desire to see much more. Consequently he resolved to journey, though he was blind as a bat. He soon became renowned as the "Blind Traveller," and the incidents of his life are extremely interesting.

Nine years after the loss of his vision, he travelled through France, Switzerland, Italy, and some other countries, without being accompanied by a guide. Subsequently he made another journey, and travelled through Russia into Liberia. At this time, he resolved to travel around the world; but the Russian authorities took him for a *spy* (as if a blind man would be sent on such an errand), and compelled him to return. He returned through Austria, Saxony, Prussia, and Hanover. In 1827, he undertook to fulfil his former resolution of going round the world.

He accomplished his purpose, and arrived at home in 1832. In 1834 he published an account of this voyage, in four octavo volumes.

The amount of information which he obtained in his travels, and the accuracy of his description of objects, was truly remarkable. Among the things in which he was particularly interested was the structure of machinery, and he says of it: "If it be inquired how I can understand the structure and action of machinery, I would ask how the machinery in question came to be originally invented. Doubtless, it would be replied, 'by man's imagination.' If so, how much easier may it be for my imagination to comprehend what has been reduced to practical demonstration, so evident that a mere operative mechanic can execute it from description only."

When he was in St. Petersburg he recognized a bust of the Emperor Alexander by the sense of touch, and was able to denote points in which it differed from one he had previously examined.

He was so easy and natural in all his movements that people were often with him some length of time before they recognized his blindness. On one occasion, he mentioned to the Governor of Tobolsk that he had visited St. Helena, when the Governor remarked that he had a drawing of that island, and immediately brought it forward, that Holman might see whether it was a faithful representation.

When on shipboard, he frequently went aloft, climbing the rigging as dextrously as those who have good eyes. On one of these occasions, when the deck was so slippery from rain that had fallen as to render a walk thereon uncomfortable, he took an excursion to the main-topmast-head. The L'ascars on board were so agitated at the sight of a blind man in that perilous situation, that they talked of following, to lash him to the rigging.

In Ceylon he went out with a party to hunt elephants, and he gives the following account of it: "It may be asked where I was during this interesting scene? In reply, I beg to acquaint my readers that I continued on horseback, as close to my friends as they would allow me, and generally contrived to be within speaking distance; for I believe that I was as fully excited, and as much interested in the sport, as any person present. Being left masters of the field, we anxiously advanced to examine the spoil, which proved to be a female of extraordinary size. *I climbed upon the carcas, where I stood and danced in triumph.*"

In travelling, he always managed his own finances; and he was so expert in recognizing coin, that he was seldom, if ever, deceived. He says, "Notwithstanding I have travelled so much in foreign countries, and have had so extensive an intercourse with strangers, I think I may safely say, that I have not been more deceived, or suffered greater losses in money transactions, than any of my countrymen."

He frequently found himself in relations where his own services were indispensable to the persons around him. His experience in this particular, was not unlike that of the blind Dr. Moyes, who was upset in a stage-coach, one dark night, in England. The coach and horses were rolled into a ditch, from which it was difficult to remove them. Neither the driver, nor the eight passengers, each of whom were supplied with a good pair of eyes, could give directions in the dark; so they yielded the management to their blind fellow-traveller, to whom the darkness and the light were alike. He who could not discern a ray of light at noon-day, placed each passenger at his post, and then ordered them to pull and lift, according to his judgment, until the horses and vehicle were extricated from their unusual position.

Such facts show that almost any thing is possible to the resolute and persevering. Perhaps there can be no greater obstacles to success than those considered in the foregoing pages; and yet, great as these obstacles are, they have been overcome. What has been done once, can be done again. Like qualities, employed in a similar way, will lead to like results. Hence, the poor and humble, the unfortunate and afflicted, may be encouraged. They need not sit down in gloomy despondency; for there is hope in their case. They have, at least, the encouraging truth to ponder, *that they can make themselves almost any thing they wish to become.*

CHAPTER XXV.

MORAL AND RELIGIOUS CHARACTER.

What has been implied—Moral sentiments in youth—Extract from his Work-house Journal—A pauper's prayer—Speaks well for Kitto's heart—Influence of his grandmother—Became a true child of God under Mr. Grove's influence—Extract from his Journal, showing the change wrought in him—Noble instance of conscientiousness—Its contrasts with certain kinds of dishonesty—Summary view.

MUCH has been implied upon this subject in previous chapters, although it has received no direct attention. We might pass it by entirely, without doing injustice to the memory of the dead; for the inference of all readers concerning his moral character, derived from what has been said, will be the same. But there are some features of his religious experience that deserve to be brought out more prominently to view.

We have seen that his excellent grandmother sought to impress wholesome moral and religious lessons upon his heart, and that he did not forget them. We have quoted extracts from his early Journal that are imbued with a noble christian spirit.

Yet it is well to view that part of his character more minutely.

When he was a youth in the work-house, he wrote in his Journal one day, as if he were addressing a a friend: —

"October 12. — Among the inconveniences of the work-house, one is that I cannot kneel when I pray, consequently I used to pray in bed, lying down, in the evenings. Now I think it was rather an irreverential posture to pray in; therefore I have been thinking of a more convenient place. To-day I began to pray in the mornings. Though deaf, I am obliged to attend morning prayers; so it occurred to me, as I am now in the men's part of the prayer-room, and as no one else sits on the chest under the window, I might make an improvement. So this morning, for the first time, at morning prayers, I turned my face to the window, and stood, inclining one knee against the chest, and made a prayer to my FATHER. It did not last quite so long as the Guardian takes to read morning prayers. I shall still continue to examine myself a little, and recommend myslf to the care of God before I go to sleep in evenings. I pray, you know, *extempore*. You say, dearest Harry, that you should like to know what I pray for. I will try to gratify you."

Then follows a prayer which is worthy of being read, penned as it was, by a pauper at sixteen years of age. Its great length is an objection to introducing it here entire, so we will give some extracts therefrom: —

"King of the Universe! I, an atom of that universe, dare humbly pray thee to incline thy ear, while at thy footstool I confess that I am a wretched sinner; that I have broken thy laws, and thy commandments I have trodden under my feet; that I have slighted thee, my Maker; that I have not done my duty to thee, my neighbor, or myself; that I have deserved nothing at thy hands but thy displeasure. I have wasted the precious moments which thou givest me to improve. I have murmured at thy decrees, because thou, in thy mercy, wast pleased to afflict me, and because thou gavest me to drink of the cup of affliction. I have not loved thee as thou oughtest to be loved. I have suffered impure desires and evil passions to influence my actions. In short, O Lord, I am a miserable, self-convicted sinner. I have deserved thy wrath and fearful indignation, and I do not remember one good action that ever I did; which makes me know that thou alone canst save me Therefore, Almighty God, overburdened as I am with sin, I dare humbly sue thee to pardon my sins; remember not against me my inquities, but blot them from the book of thy remembrance, and erase them from the tablets of thy memory. Hear me, O God, when I cry to thee for that mercy I do not deserve. Give me, most merciful Father, the gifts of thy grace. Give me repentance; for, without thy aid, I cannot repent of my sins nor abide by my purpose of leading a new life; without thy aid I cannot know myself. Give, me, Eternal King, faith, that no doubts may obtrude themselves, that I may believe in Jesus Christ, and keep thy law. Do thou also grant unto me, O Lord, content, that I may be satisfied with whatever situation in life is to be thy pleasure to assign me; and that I may be convinced that whatsoever thou doest is for my benefit; and that I may thank thee even for the rod with which thou dost chastise me."

. . . .

"Grant me, O Lord, I humbly entreat thee, grace that I may so conduct myself here on earth that, when it is thy pleasure to take me hence, I may die with a conviction that my sins are pardoned, and that at the last I may be able to exclaim, 'O death, where is thy sting; O grave, where is thy victory?'"

The sentiment and spirit of this prayer speaks well for the heart of Kitto. The influence of his grandmother is seen therein. But for her early lessons, he might not have been inclined to offer such a prayer. Probably the power of habit, formed under the eye of the good old lady, had something to do with his morning and evening devotions. For, probably, he was not a christian when he penned the above supplication, nor did he profess to be. It was not until he was brought under the influence of Mr. Groves that he experienced that change which caused him to feel that he was a true child of God. Mr. Groves was a man of deep-toned piety. A missionary spirit was his at all times, and every young person who came under his influence, felt its power. Kitto said of him, "He is not a Methodist, a Calvinist, a Lutheran, or a Papist. What, then, is he? A Deist, a Unitarian, an Antinomian? No. He is one of those rather singular characters, a Bible Christian, and a disciple of the meek and lowly Jesus; not nominally, *but practically and really such.* A man so devotedly, so fervently attached to the

Scriptures, I never knew before, and this is the best criterion I can furnish you of judging of his character and disposition."

In one of his letters to Mr. Barnard, Kitto refers to the change which he experienced, in the following words: —

"When I look back, I am surprised at the very great change which has taken place in my views since I came hither; a change which clearly convicts me, in many former instances of my life, of folly and impropriety. . . . . To what is this change to be imputed? Perhaps to a more exclusive contemplation of divine things; to a more attentive study of the Word of Life; to abstraction from many temporal things, which at Plymouth too deeply engrossed my thoughts; to my intercourse with Mr. Groves: but *chiefly*, I conclude, to the grace of God, who has at length permitted that 'day-spring from on high,' to arise, *for the appearance of which I have long prayed;* and which, when fully risen, will enable me to behold the beauty of holiness in all its glory and perfection; and, by the strengthening influence of the Holy Spirit, to pursue that light which will then be revealed more completely than at present.

"I think it is a question which every christian must necessarily, according to the principles of his faith, ask himself, how he may be usefully employed in promoting the happiness of his brethren, and in extending the kingdom, and in promulgating the knowledge of his Master. I have asked myself the question, and it appears to me that my pen is the most obvious means of attaining those ends which my deafness leaves open to me; and, to the attainment of these objects, it shall henceforth be employed, or never employed at all. Fame, emolument, honor, are now nothing to me; I have now higher objects, higher motives; and that I could ever had other designs in view by literary pursuits than those which my heart will now acknowledge, is a subject of wonder and regret."

At this time, Kitto was twenty years of age, and henceforth a new spirit seemed to animate his breast. If worldly ambition had influenced him at all in his previous aims and efforts, it ceased to control him from that time. Now his great desire was to glorify God, by doing the greatest amount of good to his fellow men. He cultivated the spirit of prayer. He made a public profession of religion, and went to the table of our Lord. In short, he lived a christian.

There is an incident on record, which illustrates his delicate conscientiousness, to which allusion was made in a former chapter. One of his publishers, who was indebted to him considerably, was on the eve of bankruptcy. Kitto was informed respecting his condition, and might have secured himself against loss, but he refused to do it, on the ground that it was wrong. He regarded his own claims on a par with the claims of others, and therefore any effort to secure his own debt would be robbing other creditors of some of their dues. This case of conscience presents such a contrast with what we frequently witness, that it becomes worthy of notice. Good men, even, do not scruple to secure their own claims upon a debtor on the eve of his failure, though other creditors, more needy than themselves, lose all they have. We have known a man of high reputation for integrity and christian principle, to accept the payment of a note from a debtor who announced to him privately, that he was bankrupt, and that he (the bankrupt) desired to secure him against loss, as a friend, before his actual condition was made public. At the same time, there were other creditors far less able to sustain a loss, and yet this man took his money, and probably considered himself fortunate. In another instance, a trader, who was about to fail, went to a creditor, who was a particular friend, stated what would soon happen, and proposed to secure him by mortgaging a certain piece of land. The offer was accepted, and this creditor got his pay; while others, poorer than himself, lost the most of their claims. Such things are quite common; so common, indeed, that they are scarcely regarded wrong. They occur among professing christians sometimes, without eliciting particular notice from their brethren.

It was against the unrighteous principle involved in such cases, that Kitto protested. Rather than stain his own soul with the guilt of such transactions, he would sacrifice the last dollar of his claim. It was a noble stand to take. None do thus declare for the right except they possess an enlighted conscience, unyielding integrity, and stern moral or religious principle.

Such was Kitto's moral and religious character: in childhood, gentle and truthful; in youth, upright and moral; in manhood, holy and christlike. It was his daily study to do right; and the smile of an approving conscience was his choicest luxury. His soul dwelt in a purer atmosphere than is breathed by the larger part of mankind. His thoughts were ever busy with the noblest and most exalted themes. He saw the hand of God in every event of life, and recognized his unseen agency even in the severest trials. His christian manhood was a crown of glory to the church.

CHAPTER XXVI.

SICKNESS AND DEATH.

Augustine said, "No man can die ill who has lived well"—Thomas Paine, the Infidel—The dying Newport—Last hour of pious Janeway—Kitto's end, peace—Account of his last sickness—A previous attack—His resolve to finish a work pledged, though he should die—Subscription by friends to secure rest for him—His daguerreotype—His departure for Germany—Death of two children there—Account of it by Mrs. Kitto—Last paragraph of Kitto's last letter—Last things of the dead—Account of his death by Mrs. Kitto—Lines by Montgomery.

IT might be expected that one who had lived so well, would endure the pangs of fatal disease with fortitude, and meet the "King of Terrors" as a spiritual conquerer. Augustine said, "No man can die ill who has lived well." The last end of the righteous confirms the truth of his remark, while the closing scene of the wicked fearfully proclaims the opposite.

Thomas Paine, who made light of religion and discarded the Bible, died as he had lived, without God, and without hope. He frequently cried out, as his end drew near, "O Lord, help me! God help! Jesus Christ help me!" He said to a neighbor who carried him some dainties, "If the devil ever had an agent on earth, I have been one." The dying Newport exclaimed: "Do I assert that there is no hell, while I feel one in my own bosom? Am I certain there is no after retribution, when I feel a present judgment? Wretch that I am, whither shall I fly from this breast? What will become of me?" A friend inquired how he did. "Damned and lost forever," he replied. His last words were, "Oh, the insufferable pangs of hell and damnation!"

These men reaped as they had sown. Their lives were characterized by high-handed rebellion against God, and their expiring moments were filled with unutterable anguish. They had lived wickedly, and they died in agony. What a painful contrast with the departure of a truly good man! Said the pious Janeway, about the time he was struck with death, "Methinks I stand, as it were, with one foot in heaven, and the other upon earth. Methinks I hear the melody of heaven; and, by faith, I see the angels waiting to carry my soul to the bosom of Jesus, and I shall be forever with the Lord in glory. And who can choose but rejoice in all this?" His life was a beautiful imitation of the life of Christ, and its last hours were consequently irradiated with light from the cross.

Kitto's life closed with similar peace and triumph. He died as he had lived — well.

On the fourth day of February, 1854, he was seized with a violent fit early in the morning, and for some time he lay insensible. At length, however, he gradually opened his eyes, and consciousness returned. At first he was somewhat startled by the bustle around him, and especially at seeing his distinguished physician, Dr. Tunaly, at his bed-side. But he soon learned the cause of so much stir.

It should be stated that, for some months, his health had been declining, and the physicians had cut down his study-hours very materially. Four or five months before, he was so ill that he consulted Dr. Bird; and, after a few weeks attendance, the Doctor said, "I cannot cure him: no medical man can. Nothing but absolute rest from immediate labor can be of service. All I can do is to endeavor to subdue the irritation of the brain, which he goes home and excites immediately, by using it." His devoted wife joined with the physician in entreating him to cease from mental effort for a while. But he replied,

"No! I must first finish the work for which I have had the money; and if I knew that I should die with the pen in my hand, I will go on as long as the Lord permits." He was permitted to finish the work; but on the following morning he had a slight attack of paralysis.

The above language of Dr. Kitto, about dying with his pen in his hand, may seem at first like utter recklessness. But the reader should take notice of the reason he gives for desiring to complete the work. He had bargained for it with his publisher, who *paid him in advance;* and, for this reason, he felt that the work must be done. It is another instance of his conscientious regard for right. Rather than fail to redeem his pledge, he would hazard health, and even life itself. Viewing the act in this light, it partakes even of the sublime. What devotion to uprightness is that which makes a sacrifice, not only of ease and comfort, but of health and life, to redeem a pledge.

Immediately after Dr. Kitto was seized with a fit, a movement commenced of raising a subscription among his friends sufficient to allow him one or two years of repose. It became very evident to his friends, and by this time Kitto himself was convinced of the fact, that excessive mental exertion had brought him to the verge of the grave. It was fully believed that nothing could save his valuable life but *rest.* The effort to raise funds for the support of himself and family, was very successful; and arrangements were made for Kitto's early departure, with his wife and seven children, to Germany. He recovered from the violent attack of February so far as to be able to leave England on the ninth day of August following. A few days before he left, an incident occurred, the account of which, in his own words, shows how cheerful was his spirit under this additional trial.

"At Shireen's (his daughter) supplication," he said, in a letter to a friend, "I sat to the sun for my portrait on Saturday. Till I saw it, I had no idea how grand I look; it seems the concentrated essence of twenty aldermen and ten bishops, all in one. Mrs. K. sat also; but woman-like, she spoke in the very crisis of the operation, and so spoiled the likeness. I amused myself much with the idea that the sun, who has hitherto lived like a gentleman, is now obliged to work for his living."

Kitto proceeded with his family to Stuttgart, where they arrived after a pleasant, though wearisome journey. A bitter experience, however, awaited them there. Death took their eldest and youngest child within a few weeks after their arrival, and Dr. Kitto himself continued to decline. Mrs. Kitto thus tells the sad tale of sorrow: —

"September twenty-first arrived, the twenty-first anniversary of our marriage-day, which, on former occasions, had been devoted to a little relaxation and amusement with the children. But here we were, I with my last babe dying in my arms — poor Shireen, our first-born, confined to her bed, dying in the next room — and dear Kitto had wandered to Stuttgart (they had just removed to Connstatt), in search of some trifle to present to me, according to his custom. On giving it to me, he remarked that he felt it was very inappropriate to either of our states of feeling then, but, in all probability, it was the last he should give me. Our babe died. Three weeks passed on, during which dear Shireen never rose, and it was quite evident she was fast approaching the other world; but her hopes were on this, and she did not express herself as having any idea of the really critical position she was in. We had both been desirous that she should feel that her change was near; but how were we to tell her? I felt I could not. Her dear father read and talked to her, and gave some gentle hints that the doctors would not be answerable for the results, and, indeed, that they thought it a critical case. Whilst we were hesitating thus to communicate with her, the Lord himself showed his intentions towards her. One morning, as I was attending to her, she said, 'Mamma, I dreamed last night that the dean of the place came and told me I was only to live a fortnight.' I took advantage of the opportunity as well as I was able, and said to her, 'Well, my dear, the Lord speaks in various ways, and perhaps this is his message to you.' 'Yes,' she said, 'I think it is; for certainly I cannot live long thus.' After this she became quite resigned and composed, and daily talked very sweetly on the subject of her decease, both with her dear father and myself. She died exactly at the end of the fortnight, as her dream had told her. Now all was silence and sadness. She, on whom so many bright hopes had been fixed, had left us; and we passed and met each other in silence, neither being able to comfort, or willing to distress the other. He was moved to tears when he saw the myrtle wreath which was to deck the brow, now in corruption, of our once lovely child. It is a custom here thus to crown a young unmarried female, as with us a wreath of orange blossoms adorns a bride. The idea may be pretty, but the feelings produced in us at the sight of the poor, pallid face thus adorned, were distressing indeed. Dear Kitto was very particular in the choice of a site for our beloved daughter's grave. He wanted it amongst old things, he said, for he hated new things, adding that he should have a grave for himself by her side, as now he did not intend to leave Connstatt unless he got well."

These repeated bereavements were a heavy blow to Kitto in his feeble state, and his decline was, in consequence, more rapid. Yet he was calm and submissive, and looked forward to the period of his own dissolution with childlike trust and cheerful hope. The last paragraph of the last letter he ever penned contained these words: "But, though heart-smitten, I have not been allowed to sorrow as having no hope; and I begin to perceive that, by these variously afflictive dispensations, my Lord is calling me up thither, to the higher room in which he sits, that I may see more of his grace, and that I may more clearly understand the inner mysteries of his kingdom. What more awaits me, I guess not. But the

Lord's will be done." There is always something of peculiar interest about the last thing that a departed friend did. We remember it through our whole life. His last word or look even, is impressed indelibly upon the heart. To possess the last letter he ever wrote, this is a precious privilege. To learn therefrom the nature of his thoughts and feelings, when he held a pen for the last time, this, too, is congenial. In the above extract we have the last words that Kitto penned; and they show that he was fast ripening for heavenly mansions. In less than four weeks from that time, he bowed his head to the destroyer, and his spirit took its everlasting flight. The closing scene is touchingly described by Mrs. Kitto: —

"Two mornings before he was finally taken from us, he was talking to me, and said, 'Somehow I begin to feel a sad distaste of life; I am now in a useless state, with little hope, that I can see, of ever being useful again.' He added, 'I, who have all my life been in the habit of referring every thing to God, naturally sit and ask myself what all these things mean; and endeavor, if possible, to find out what his mind towards me is; and, unless it be to draw me to himself, I confess I am at a loss. . . . .

He sat reading till eleven o'clock, and seemed quite pleased that I had been able to rest so long listening to him. He then retired for the night. About three o'clock in the morning I was awakened by his step in the room. I immediately sprang up, and inquired what was the matter. He said, 'unless I can be sick, I feel I shall be very ill.' I applied some remedies which had the desired effect, and wished to send for Dr. Burkhardt, his medical attendant, but he would not allow me, saying, it would pass off. I did not feel any particular alarm, and he went again to bed, and slept till about seven, when I inquired how he was. He said he felt better, and asked for his *sawerwasser*. He then rose and dressed himself, but said he would defer the more laborious process of shaving and washing till he had taken his breakfast. He sat at the table with the children and myself. As soon as they had gone to school, he said, 'Well, after all, I think I must have a very strong constitution to stand what I have gone through. I never felt so conscious as last night of the approach of a fit; and, had I not been sick, I am sure that I should have had one.' Then, making two or three circles with his finger, to signify giddiness, he added, almost in the same breath, 'Look sharp, Bell!' I saw he was greatly affected, and caught hold of him, calling loudly to the servants, whom I hurried off to call Dr. Burckhardt, and our kind friend, Mr. Hirsch, who had shown himself throughout most anxious to render every assistance in his power. Dear Kitto, seeing I was greatly agitated, waved his hand gently up and down, signifying to me to be composed. His chest heaved violently, and continued doing so at intervals of about half an hour. Between the paroxysms he kept trying his eyes, his fingers, and his tongue, and said, 'My impression is, I shall die.' Medicine was given, but it could not be retained. He sat in his chair with his feet in a mustard bath, and leaches on his temples; and, after an interval of some hours, he was bled in the foot. There seemed, however, no signs of amendment. About two o'clock in the day he was removed to bed. But the chest kept constantly heaving, and the head was swollen, and the face very red. Stertorous breathing commenced, and it became very difficult to understand him; all told too plainly that, in a few hours, we should be left desolate. In the early part of the evening he said, 'I am being choaked. Is it death?' I spoke with my fingers, but I saw that he could not make out what I said. I then, with my head, signified that it was. He added, 'Pray to God to take me soon.' These were his last words. He continued for some hours in this agony, which no human power could alleviate. Mr. Hirsch, and other kind friends, offered to set with us during the night; but all help of man was vain. Towards five o'clock the convulsive struggle became too agonizing to witness, and Dr. Burckhardt, who had been sent for, insisted upon my retiring, and would not suffer me again to return. I never saw him afterwards. About seven o'clock I was told that all was over, and that my beloved husband had entered into the rest prepared for the people of God."

He was laid beside his departed children in the cemetery at Connstatt. The country that gave him birth has not the honor of guarding his remains; but his memory is there enshrined in the hearts of thousands. Over his grave an appropriate slab has been erected by the publisher of his last work — a grateful tribute to the talents and worth of one, whose life was pure, and whose end was peace.

> " Go to the grave in all thy glorious prime,
> In full activity of zeal and power;
> A Christian cannot die before his time;
> The Lord's appointment is the servant's hour.

"Go to the grave; at noon from labor cease;
  Rest on thy sheaves, thy harvest task is done;
Come from the heart of battle, and in peace,
  Soldier, go home; with thee the fight is won.

"Go to the grave; though like a fallen tree,
  At once with verdure, flowers, and fruit are crown'd,
Thy form may perish, and thine honors be
  Lost in the moulding bosom of the ground.

"Go to the grave, which, faithful to its trust,
  The germ of immortality shall keep;
While safe, as watched by cherubim, thy dust
  Shall, till the judgment-day, in Jesus sleep.

"Go to the grave; for there thy Saviour lay
  In death's embraces, ere he rose on high;
And all the ransomed, by that norrow way,
  Pass to eternal life beyond the sky.

"Go to the grave; — no! take thy seat above;
  Be thy pure spirit present with the Lord,
Where thou, for faith and hope, hast perfect love,
  And open vision for the written Word."

CHAPTER XXVII.

MAN PROPOSES, GOD DISPOSES.

The hand of God in Kitto's life—One fault of history and biography—God raises up agents for great works—Moses—Martin Luther—So with Kitto—Incidents which show the hand of God in his life—Poverty, accident, calamity, affliction, disappointments, all necessary to fit him for his work—Lives of great men often singularly preserved amid perils—Case of John Bunyan—Isaac Newton—Kitto saw and acknowledged Providence in his career, before he died.

HIGH authority has said, "A man's heart deviseth his way; but the Lord directeth his steps." Unless the reader beholds the hand of God in such a life as Kitto's, it loses much of its significance and power. One great fault of mankind is, that they live without seeing God in the affairs of life. If we look into our histories, we find that they are written just as if there were no God, and man the sole manager of temporal concerns. How much more interesting and impressive they would be, if the hand of God was recognized therein! A faithful history of the past shows that human enterprises have been frustrated, and human wickedness overruled, to advance the truth; that all things have, on the whole, been so controlled as to further Christianity. Why should not historians keep in view this important fact when executing their work? Their labors would certainly be turned to much better account, and history would be regarded, as it really is, the record of Divine Providence.

The same remark may be made of biography. We are too little disposed to recognize God directing our steps, or the steps of others. We behold men living and acting, and read their written lives when they are dead and gone, without even noticing that God has had anything to do with their existence. Yet it is quite generally admitted, that man only "deviseth his way," while "the Lord directeth his steps." This truth is so generally admitted, that it has passed into the proverb, "Man proposes, God disposes." Why not give prominence so this fact in writing the lives of men and women?

In past ages, when God has been about to perform some great work, he has prepared his agent for the enterprise. He has selected men, and qualified them, by his own peculiar discipline, for the work in view. For example, a renowned legislator and leader was needed in Israel. There was no man competent to rule over God's chosen people, for the reason that none had enjoyed the necessary dicipline. From whence should help arise? All the male children in the land were doomed to destruction by Pharaoh, in order to prevent the reign of a mighty man among his foes. But God, nevertheless, trains the man. A mother is moved to hide her new-born child until it is a few months old, and its cries can be heard by the eagle-eyed officials. Then she carefully prepares an ark of rushes, which is deposited among the flags in the river of Egypt. Pharaoh's daughter repairs thither to bathe. She sees something floating on the water, and she orders her maids to bring it. She opens the basket, and behold, it is a child. She understands at once that it is a device of some loving mother to spare the child which her father had doomed to death. Her woman's heart is moved to pity; and she resolves to spare the little one. God inclines her to seek a nurse, and, at the same time, orders things so that the child's own mother becomes the nurse. This was just what was necessary. Nearly all great men are trained by faithful mothers. A mother's influence was needed to rear a leader in Israel. Now look at the picture. There is the child Moses, being reared under the patronage of the very king, whose cruel edict had doomed him to die. God so ordered affairs that the ruler, who studied to hinder the rise of mighty foes, should rear the mightiest of all in his own proud Court. He devised his way, but God directed his steps. Pharaoh proposed, but God disposed. He grew up under royal patronage, acquiring just the knowledge that was necessary for the place he was to fill, and having such an experience as was indispensable to a wise legislator. How conspicuous is the hand of God in his eventful history!

Again, when God was about to convulse the world with what men call "the Great Reformation," he took a little boy who was gathering sticks with his mother at the mines of Mansfield, and disciplined him to perform the needful human agency. His father, though a poor man, was moved to send his son to school, after having subjected him to strict religious culture first under his own roof. At fourteen years of age, he was in the school of the Franciscans, at Magdeburg, so extremely poor that he was obliged to spend his play-hours in singing from door to door for his bread. It was then common for the poor, who were singers, to perform in this way from house to house, as it is now for hand-organists. The boy's thirst for knowledge increased as obstacles rose in his path. One day, after he had been turned away from several doors without bread, and he was saying to himself, "Must I, for the want of bread, leave my studies, and return to the mines of Mansfield?" a door suddenly opened, and a good woman, having pity on the "beggar boy," invited him to come in. But for this timely aid, he might have left his books forever. God seems to have raised up this woman to aid in training the great Reformer; for, from this time, she became his patroness, and he was soon in the University of Erfurth, the brightest of all the students. He designed to study law; but God had another purpose in view. One day he was in the Library of the University, where he spent his leisure moments, and he found a new and strange book — the Bible. Though twenty years of age, he had never seen a Bible before. He read it, was convicted of sin, and resolved to live for God. Believing that he could be holy only in the seclusion of a monastery, he hurried within, where he learned that there was no power in monastic life to regenerate the heart. This was the experience he needed, in order to fit him to become a reformer in those days. With this rigid discipline, so marked with the wisdom and counsel of God, Luther went forth to duty in the world; and the world has acknowledged his power.

God's hand is thus seen in the lives of men. It is no less conspicuous in the chequered experience of Kitto. It is when we view his life in this higher relation, and see the hand of God directing affairs so as to make him an agent of the greatest good to his fellow-men, that we are most impressed by his character.

Mark some of the incidents of his life. Consider, however, in the first place, that such work as Kitto performed, in the field of Biblical Science, was greatly needed at the time. It was comparatively a new field of mental effort, and the right man was needed for the work. God followed his usual plan, and went to the poor and humble for an instrument. John Kitto is compelled to leave his home on account of its poverty and wretchedness, that a pious grandmother might beget and foster a love of truth and learning in his heart. He must know, from bitter experience, what poverty is, that he may be content to do the work which the Lord has assigned him, for only his daily bread, and scarcely that; for this is all the world will give. He must not love social converse too much, and his mind must be disposed to toil patiently and perseveringly upon neglected subjects, to prepare such works as those of which he became the author. Many scholars cannot sufficiently abstract themselves from the world, to perform this labor with success. Perhaps Kitto will not do it. Ah, yes! Providence has provided the way. The aged grandmother is made ill, so that the lad is obliged to return to his father's miserable abode. There is such poverty there, too, that Kitto must aid his father, and carry tiles to the top of a house, though he is small for the work. With a load upon his back, he falls from the roof upon the pavement below, and is made forever deaf. Now he is shut out from the world. He is compelled to retire within himself, and find his pleasure in *thought.* Perhaps this calamity was needed, in order to fit him for the close application necessary to perform his life-mission well. Without it, he might not have undertaken such a task. A deaf man is certainly the best qualified, physically, for such patience-trying labor.

But how shall he acquire an education? He must first be sent to the Poor-house. A "learned pauper" will soon attract public notice. Soon he will find benefactors, drawn to him by the novelty of his condition. *Deafness* and *pauper* are two words that will move the public mind. Especially will this be the case if he can give some more decided demonstration of his talents. He can: a way is provided. He is apprenticed to a cruel wretch, who abuses him. He seeks deliverance from his merciless employer. His case goes into court. He is obliged to write a statement of it. It is done with such ability that the court is surprised. Henceforth it is told abroad that the poor, deaf pauper has remarkable talents. Benefactors arise. He is taken from the Poor-house, and placed where he can enjoy intellectual advantages. Strange as it may seem, he is soon sent by his professed literary benefactors to learn the art of dentistry. God meant thereby to fit him for the missionary field. Mr. Groves, the dentist, is a man of God, and his influence brings Kitto directly to the cross. Henceforth he only asks to be useful. Then he goes to Islington, to learn the art of printing, without time to study, except that which he abstracts from the hours of sleep. It looks as if his benefactors had become tired of supporting him, and hereafter would have him work at a trade. He is disheartened. But God's hand is in it. He has something for Kitto to learn in Malta. To Malta he is sent as a printer, where he remains till God has opened the way to a more important field. He returns with the intention of devoting himself to literary pursuits. He expects to go no more abroad. After his return he goes to visit Mr. Groves, the pious dentist, whom he loves, to bid him farewell as he leaves for a distant missionary field. Contrary to his expectation, instead of bidding him adieu, he agrees to accompany him to Bagdad, as a missionary. He goes thither, and remains more than three years. His experience in foreign lands has made him acquainted with Oriental manners and customs, without which knowledge he could not have prepared the volumes which he afterwards wrote. He returns from Bagdad, when the Society for the Diffusion of Knowledge are in want of editorial talent. He is just the man needed, and is engaged. He enters upon those literary labors in which we have seen that he became distinguished. Several years before, he was betrothed to a young lady; but, after he went to Malta, she married another man. It was a heavy blow to him, and he viewed it as a great affliction. But God meant it for good; for this lady proved anything but a sensible, valuable woman; while Kitto subsequently found and married a lady who was a model in all that pertains to domestic duties, and, as we have seen, rendered him important service in his literary pursuits.

The hand of God is as distinctly seen in this life of Kitto, as in the history of Joseph or Moses. He was led in a way that he knew not, all his life long. The life of Joseph was not more singularly preserved than was that of Kitto. It was almost a miracle that the latter was saved from immediate death when he fell from the roof. But his life-work was not done; yea, it was scarcely begun. Again in Malta, the steed on which he rode became unmanageable one day, and he was thrown off upon the stones, and taken up for dead. In a little while, however, he opened his eyes; for God had a great work for him to do. It is a remarkable fact that great and good men, at some period of life, are singularly saved from death. John Bunyan was twice saved from the most imminent danger of drowning; and, when serving under Oliver Cromwell, at the siege of Leicester, a comrade voluntarily took his place as sentinel, and was shot dead at his post. Bunyan would have shared the same fate but for this exchange. But he was a chosen vessel of God, though a wicked man when thus preserved. In like manner, John Newton was watched over by unseen eyes when calamity and disease were near. He was proverbially punctual; yet, one day he was detained by some business so that he did not get to his boat until much later than usual. On his return, he started out in his boat, as heretofore, to inspect a ship, but the ship blew up before he reached her. If he had not been detained, he would have perished with those on board. Those who are to act a conspicuous part for the church are often thus preserved from destruction.

A life like Kitto's becomes nobler and grander when we thus trace the hand of God in his career. In a most emphatic sense, he becomes a child of Providence; just as really under the guidance of Jehovah, as Abraham or Moses.

In his riper years, Kitto saw and acknowledged the hand of God in every event of his life. He had passed through scenes of darkness and perplexity, and experienced much that he called mysterious at the time, but he lived to see it all cleared up, and the name of his God glorified. There were times when his heart was sad over disappointed hopes; but ere he went to his rest, he saw that all things had worked together for his good.

> "There's a Divinity that shapes our ends,
> Rough-hew them as we will."

CHAPTER XXVIII.

CONCLUSION.

The Title of this Volume—Reasons for it—The reader now familiar with a remarkable life—Personal exertions, and not gifts, made Kitto—Extracts from a "Critical Estimate of Kitto's Life and Writings," by Professor Eadie, to confirm the foregoing views—Lines by Longfellow.

"FROM POOR-HOUSE TO PULPIT!" methinks I hear the reader exclaim: "where and when did Dr. Kitto fill a pulpit?" "What authority for this title of the book?" We are not surprised that these inquiries should be made. These questions may be honestly asked: we will honestly answer them.

First. Kitto would have entered the sacred office, as advised by many friends, but for his deafness. He considered this affliction so much of a hindrance to success in the ministry, that he concluded he could do the greatest good with his pen.

Second. He did become a lay missionary, and rendered five years of useful service in the cause. He possessed the spirit and energy of a faithful herald of the cross.

Third. He devoted the best part of his life to Biblical studies, and was the author of several works very useful to ministers, and students of the Scriptures generally. He also wrote, as we have seen, eight volumes of Bible Illustrations, which are no other than so many short sermons of an excellent character, for the use of families. His pen was continually employed in defence of the truth.

Fourth. In consideration of his Biblical and Theological learning and labors, a German University conferred upon him the degree of Doctor of Divinity. No preacher was ever more deserving of the degree D.D. He possessed every attainment, and performed every labor which is usually considered necessary to the possession of this honorable title, except proclaiming the gospel with the living voice. He did proclaim the gospel with his pen. He reached more hearts, by a thousand fold, in this way of preaching the truth, than he could have done as a pastor. At any period in the latter years of his life, he might have stepped into the pulpit to preach the truth, and found a plenty of joyful hearers to welcome him as an able and good ambassador for Christ. He was, indeed, a minister of the Word. His pulpit was his writing desk; his sermons went forth on the printed page; and his congregation was the Christian world.

For these reasons, Kitto should be classed with the ministers of Christ. There is no other class of professional men with whom he can so well be ranked. He was more than a student. He was more than a Biblical scholar. He was more than an author. He was a defender of the truth; an expounder of the Bible; an able commentator; a preacher of righteousness. This is a sufficient vindication of the title of this volume.

The reader has now been made acquainted with a remarkable life. The leading elements of it have been enumerated, so that it is not difficult to see *why* and *how* a boy so humble, became a man so learned and loved. He might have been well endowed by nature, and yet, personal exertion alone worked out his remarkable destiny. This was always his own opinion of his success. He never regarded his mental endowments as superior. He wrote to Mr. Woolcombe, at the age of twenty-three, "I have no peculiar talent, and do not want it; it would do me more harm than good. I only think that I have a certain degree of *industry*, which, *applied to its proper object*, may make me an instrument of usefulness, of greater usefulness, perhaps, than *mere talent* can enable any man to effect."

We cannot conclude this volume more appropriately than by quoting from a "Critical Estimate of Dr. Kitto's Life and Writings," by Professor Eadie, of Glasgow, some extracts which confirm the views we have just advanced, as well as those recorded on other pages.

"The name of Dr. Kitto is now immortally associated with Biblical study and literature. The measure of his success is not more amazing in its amount than in the means by which he reached it. His life is as instructive as are his labors; and, both combined, present an unequalled picture of triumph over obstacles which have been very rarely so surmounted, and over circumstances which few have ventured to encounter, and which fewer still have mastered to such advantage. For he did not merely neutralize the adverse position of his earlier years, but he wrung from it the lessons and habits which slowly built up his fame, as they prepared him for his ultimate achievements. Truly has he realized the riddle of Samson — "Out of the eater came forth meat, and out of the strong came forth sweetness." What a contrast between the deaf and pauper boy of 1819, wheedled into a work-house to keep him from "hunger and fasting, cold and nakedness," and the John Kitto of 1854, doctor of theology, though a layman member of the Society of Antiquities, Editor of the Pictorial Bible and the Cyclopædia of Biblical Literature, and author of the Daily Bible Illustrations. The interval between the two extremes was long, and sometimes very gloomy; yet he bore bravely up, with earnest resolution, and strong faith in God, as if he had often murmured to himself: —

> "Be still, sad heart, and cease repining;
> Behind the clouds the sun is shining;
> Thy fate is the common fate of all —
> Into each life some rain must fall,
> Some days must be dark and dreary."

. . . .

"What he did, he did with his might. It was not a feat, and done with it, but patient and protracted industry. He did not spring to his prey, like the lion, but he performed his daily task like the ox. He did his work with considerable ease; but he was always at his work. He was either fishing, or mending his nets; either composing, or preparing for composition. From his earliest days he could not be idle; his repose was in activity. The swallow feeds and rests on the wing. Though under the presure of a calamity which would have broke the fortitude of many, he resolved, not so much to be famous, as to be useful; and though many Providences seemed conspiring to thwart him, he boldly acted out his resolution. He often felt exhausted, and sometimes disspirited, on the rugged and up-hill path. But though faint, he was still pursuing. Every time he fell, he rose with renewed vigor. His stout heart and indomitable perseverance carried him through."

. . . .

"If one thing failed, he tried another; the conclusion of one labor was the beginning of another; either covering people's feet in Plymouth, or repairing their mouths in Exeter; setting types in Malta, or nursing and tutoring little children in Bagdad; writing for the Penny Magazine at Islington; editing the Cyclopædia at Woking, or completing the cycle with the Daily Illustration at Camden Town. His letters to myself teemed with projects to occupy him when this last work should be concluded; and they were all more or less connected with Eastern life or Biblical Illustration. His industry was unceasing from the period when his thrifty grandame taught her quiet and delicate charge to sew patchwork and kettle-holders, to the period when he felt the week by far too short to turn out in it the expected and necessary amount of copy. He liked to have his hands full, and they were sometimes too full; it puzzled him what to do first, though the indispensable penny had often summarily to settle the question."

. . . .

"Take him all in all, he was a rare phenomenon; an honor, also, to his age and country. He struggled manfully, and gained the victory; nay, out of his misfortune he constructed the steps of his advancement. Neither poverty, nor deafness, nor hard usage, nor ominous warnings, nor sudden checks, nor unpropitious commencements, nor abandoned schemes, chilled the ardor of his sacred ambition. He lived not to a long age, but he had not lived in vain; and when death at length came, it was but the Master, saying as of old, "Ephphatha, be opened!" and his spirit, which had so long dwelt in distressing silence, burst away to join the hymning myriads, whose song is

"Louder than the thunder's roar,
Or the fulness of the sea
When it breaks upon the shore."

"Tell me not in mournful numbers,
Life is but an empty dream;
For the soul is dead that slumbers,
And things are not what they seem.

Life is real! Life is earnest!
And the grave is not its goal.
'Dust thou art, to dust returnest,'
Was not spoken of the soul.

Not enjoyment, and not sorrow,
Is our destined end or way;
But to act, that each to-morrow
Find us farther than to-day.

Art is long, and Time is fleeting,
And our hearts, though stout and brave,
Still, like muffled drums, are beating
Funeral marches to the grave.

In the world's broad field of battle,
In the bivouac of Life,
Be not like dumb, driven cattle!
Be a hero in the strife!

Trust no future, howe'er pleasant!
Let the dead Past bury its dead!
Act; — act in the living Present!
Heart within, and God o'erhead!

Lives of great men all remind us
We can make our lives sumblime;
And departing, leave behind us
Footprints on the sands of time.

Footprints that perhaps another,
  Sailing o'er life's solemn main,
A forlorn and shipwrecked brother,
  Seeing, shall take heart again.

Let us then, be up and doing,
  With a heart for any fate ;
Still achieving, still pursuing,
  Learn to labor and to wait."

www.ingramcontent.com/pod-product-compliance
Lightning Source LLC
LaVergne TN
LVHW010153110826
845151LV00002B/508

* 9 7 8 1 4 2 5 5 3 6 8 0 0 *